THE 12 VOLT DOCTOR'S ALTERNATOR BOOK

by Edgar J. Beyn

SPA CREEK INC.
ANNAPOLIS, MARYLAND

Published by Spa Creek Inc.
612 Third Street
Annapolis, MD 21403
(301) 267 - 6565

ISBN 0-911551-10-7

INTRODUCTION

Alternators are all around us. There is hardly an engine which does not have one, running alongside in cars, trucks, buses, recreational vehicles, boats, aircraft, farm machines, earth moving equipment, and all kinds of stationary engines. Obviously, the alternators are doing their job very well since we hear so little about them.

And if something does go wrong, most of the more popular models have their replacement available almost instantly, waiting on dealer shelves, in alternator shops, often even in department stores.

How different things become though if you want something slightly out of the ordinary, an alternator with greater output, some added feature, unusual application, or if you and your vehicle or vessel happen to be in a place where technical services are less abundant. Where you are the available technical service. Or when you want your alternator to do something new or different and, even though the expert may have told you it could'nt be done, you are not quite ready to give up.

On top of that, it does not help that alternators on their way from the manufacturer to the engine or car factory take on a new name : a Delco alternator may become a Buick or Perkins, a Motorola one may become known as a Volvo or Universal. Just try to find a Hitachi or Mitsubishi alternator in an auto store : there it may only be known as a Mazda, while at an engine dealer's it may be called Westerbeke or Yanmar.

This book tries to make you see how alternators work, what they have in common, and how they differ in some details. The sketches should help to identify brands and types, if not models. And the dimensions should help when you have to replace one with another. If you are lucky, you will never need the trouble shooting and emergency repair instructions. But if you do, I hope they help. They should at least make you more fluent on the subject.

Your letters with comments or specific questions are welcome : leave space for notes and sketches.

Annapolis, April 1986   Edgar Beyn

CONTENTS

Introduction	iii
Names : Generator – Alternator, Difference	2
Coils and Magnets	3
Why Not Permanent Magnets	7
Of Rotor Poles and Stator Coils	10
The Stator	11
Alternating Current	12
Three Phase Alternating Current	14
Intermediate Summary	17
Rectifying Diodes	19
The Three Phase Rectifying Circuit	26
Rectifying Diodes : Mechanical	27
Auxiliary Diodes	28
Isolating Diode	29
Voltage Regulators	31
Type P and Type N	37
Excitation	40
Battery	43
Wiring Diagrams, Schematics	46
Voltage Regulator Testing : in Operation	48
Test Regulator Separately	49
Voltage Regulator and Battery Charging	50
Voltage Regulator Setting	51
Manual Alternator Controls	54
Specific Voltage Regulators	59
Repairs, Trouble Shooting	79
Alternator Output Test, Field Current Test	80
Voltage Regulator Setting Test	83
Testing Alternator Off Engine	84
Disassembling the Alternator	92
Emergency Repairs	102
Alternator Dimensions	114
Alternator File	116 – 216
INDEX	218

NAMES : GENERATOR - ALTERNATOR

Have you wondered what the difference is or which might be the proper name ? Our subject is a generator. But just as with "light bulbs" which properly should be called "lamps", the popular name alternator is now in common use. The story behind it is the change, in the early sixties, from a generator with big coils and brushes but very modest.output to a new machine of different design. It was then called a Self-Rectifying AC Generator and some other complicated names. Improvements were made in rapid succession and the new machine needed a new name because it was much different from the old. Even though some makers still avoid calling it anything but a generator, the name alternator has become official for the new design.

THE DIFFERENCE

Direct current generators have at least two brushes in contact with a commutator : a ring of copper contacts. The generated current has to flow from the copper contacts to the brushes which had to be big to carry high current. Most alternators still have brushes, but for a different purpose, to carry a few Ampere of field current. Main feature of alternators is that the power generating coils of wire are fixed in one place instead of rotating. That improvement over the conventional generators has been made possible by solid state silicon rectifiers : since the stationary generating coils produce alternating current or AC, this alternating current must first be converted to direct current before it can be used to charge a battery. Very compact but powerful silicon diodes are located directly within the alternator housings and are solidly connected directly to the power generating coils . Details in the following sections will show you how that works.

COILS AND MAGNETS

Induction is the phenomenon which makes an electric pulse appear in a wire when magnetism changes in the vicinity of the wire. The emphasis is on "change" : a pulse is generated when the magnetic field becomes stronger or weaker or changes poles. You will remember most of this ,

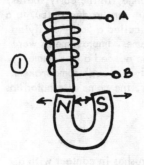

and we should just mention that the magnetism can come from permanent magnets or electromagnets, that a pulse is a momentary voltage which can create a momentary current : power. Our first design at left shows a wire coil around a bar of iron. More turns of the wire give higher voltge at the terminals A and B when the magnet is moved back and forth. Moving the horseshoe magnet back and forth is not very practical. Easier is to rotate a bar magnet as in our second design.

When a North pole passes the coil, a pulse appears at terminals A and B , and when a South pole passes next, another pulse appears at A and B but in the opposite direction. If A is plus at first, it will be minus with the next pulse and then plus again : alternating current is being generated.

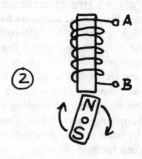

The iron bar is not only convenient to hold the wire coil, it also serves to collect and orient the magnetic field of the magnet and improves the induction effect. Even better is our third design with the coil wound on a U shaped iron core which collects as much of the magnetic field as possible by extending all the way from North to South pole of the magnet. When the magnet is rotated on the axis, induction occurs in the coil.

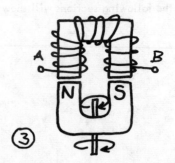

Now let's improve our design one step at a time. We will stay with the bar magnet as in sketch ② to make the next point : in that design we had only one generating coil. An improvement is to have two coils

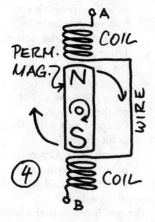

PERM.
MAG.?

A
COIL

WIRE

N
O
S

④

COIL

B

as in sketch ④ , each has a magnet pole passing by at the same time. To increase output voltage, we have both coils connected in series. At one instant, the voltage peak of one coil is added to that of the other coil. One thing to watch out for : both coils must have the wire wound in the same direction so that pulses are generated in the same direction or polarity.

What about polarity ? Look at sketch ⑤ : the North pole of a magnet is moving in to the low end of a coil as in ⑤ a . Let us assume that the coil is wound to have this make the top terminal plus as sketched. Moving the North pole away will generate a pulse with minus at the top terminal as at b . Moving a South pole in toward the same coil as at c will again have minus at the top terminal, and the opposite again

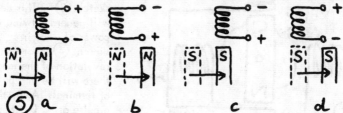

⑤ a   b   c   d

when that pole is moved away. If you look at our design in sketch ③ again, you will note that the two poles at opposite ends of the same curved coil generate pulses in the same direction which then amplify each other, the same effect as that from a stronger magnet. Sketched as the coils above, the the generator of sketch ③ would look like sketch ⑥ : opposite magnet poles moving together but at opposite ends of the same coil.

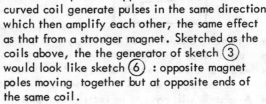

⑥

All of that is easier to sort out if you think about the way in which a permanent magnet attracts a piece of soft iron : opposite poles attract each other, and as the magnet approaches, the soft iron becomes magnetic and also formes poles. Soft iron means any iron or steel which will not become permanently magnetic. In sketch ⑦ , the poles of a magnet with solid letters is shown near a bar

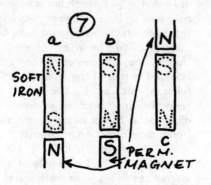

of soft iron which has become magnetic as indicated by the dotted letter poles. Note that the North and South poles at ⑦ b and c have the same effect on the iron bar. Compare this with the poles shown in sketch ⑥ . Opposite poles at opposite ends of the same coil will increase the magnetic flux and emphasize each others effect.

Next step : look at sketch ④ again. We can improve that design by having four coils instead of just two. As before, we will connect

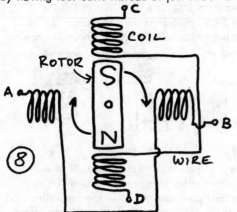

two coils in series, the ones which are at opposite ends of the magnet, sketch ⑧ . This design will generate twice the power of that in sketch ④ : for each revolution of the magnet, there will be one pulse at terminals A B, then a pulse at C D, then at A B again except with opposite polarity, then at C D with opposite polarity. We have to make a point here. Obviously it is an improvement to arrange as many coils as possible all the way around the rotating magnet. Why is there a problem with that concept ? With our bar magnet as the rotor, pulses are generated in the coils at different times. The output at A and B will have to be rectified separately from the output of C and D , only then can the direct current output be connected to common DC output terminals. With each additional pair of coils, an additional pair of rectifying diodes would become necessary. We will see how an improved rotor will simplify this complication.

To make this important point clearer, consider sketch ⑨ which has eight coils arranged around a rotating permanent magnet. Since each coil will

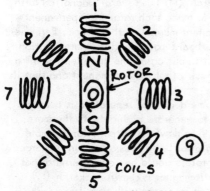

generate pulses of alternating current, the coil output must be recified or converted to direct current with diodes. As in the previous examples, we can again connect pairs of coils in series : the coils which are at the poles of the rotating magnet at the same time. We can connect in series coils 1 and 5, 2 and 6, 3 and 7, 4 and 8. But we can not connect the pairs together, their output must be rectified first which requires two diodes each, or a total of 8. This points to our next improvement, of the magnetic rotor. The same even number of generating coils in sketches ⑩ and ⑪ show two different magnetic rotors. The coils in ⑩ at best can be wired in three separate groups of two coils, the same coils with the new rotor in

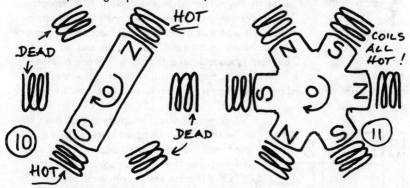

sketch ⑪ can all be wired together and then require only one set of rectifying diodes. The reason is that here all coils generate their pulse at the same time because all have a rotor magnet pole pass by at the same time. The coils can be wired in series for highest voltage, or in parallel for highest current. The alternators in real life are made with heavy wire and few turns per coil, but then have many such coils wired in series, to allow high current but at sufficiently high voltage. We will see in a moment exactly how that is done and what other tricks are used in the designs.

WHY NOT PERMANENT MAGNETS ?

Our new and improved rotor in sketch ⑪ has several magnetic North and South poles. It would be easy to make such rotor from permanent magnets or to make a single permanent magnet in that shape. Permanent magnets are used for example in outboard motors and magneto ignition systems to generate electricity. But in our case, the main feature of a permanent magnet is also its drawback : that it is permanent and that its magnetism cannot be switched off.

In the alternators, at least some degree of regulation is needed : the more capable the alternator is to generate high output, the more important it becomes to be able to turn down its output , for example when the alternator is kept running after batteries have been recharged. As attractive as permanent magnet rotors would be, our alternator has an electromagnet instead. An electromagnet is shown in sketch ⑫ .

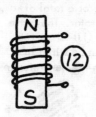

It consists of an iron core with a coil of wire wound around it. When direct current flows through the wire, the core becomes a magnet, with North and South poles at its ends. It becomes stronger with increased current and looses almost all of its magnetism when the current is interrupted. Such electromagnet is used for example in electric door bells where it attracts and releases the clapper as it switches its own coil current on and off.

The core is made from soft iron or a grade of steel which will not become a permanent magnet. In the alternator rotor, some small level of so called residual magnetism can be desireable as we will see later on .

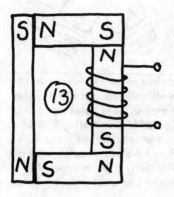

Interesting about magnets is that their North and South poles close to pieces of iron create magnetic poles in the iron . See the electromagnet in sketch ⑬ : it turns the rectangular pieces of iron into magnets which have North and South poles as shown in the sketch and which attract each other , as opposite poles are known to do. The magnetic field, instead of spreading out into space from the ends of the magnet, prefers to follow the iron pieces which contain or conduct the magnetic flux .

Patience please, follow this one step further : if we place two iron bars across the ends of the magnet in sketch ⑭ , the bars develop two new

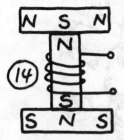

North and South poles . Very similarly, we generate the needed poles at the edge of the alternator rotor with a single electromagnet . In sketch ⑭ , we are splitting the magnetic flux into two channels to form two North poles which will not be as strong as the original N pole of the electromagnet . To make the number of magnet poles of the alternator rotor sufficiently strong, a

strong electromagnet is made with a so called field coil which is placed around the alternator shaft as in sketch ⑮ . Instead of the few turns

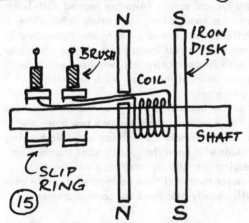

in the sketch, the field coil typically has a few hundred turns of magnet wire which is a solid copper wire with a thin coating of lacquer or varnish as insulation, made to allow maximum number of turns and minimum space taken up by insulation.

The field coil is faced by two steel disks which, if they were left as in the sketch, would develop North and

South poles at their edges as shown here. In reality, the edges of these disks are shaped to have star like extensions which form individual North and South poles , bent so that they form the outer edge of the rotor. Current for the field coil is supplied through carbon brushes which are in contact with insulated smooth copper rings which are called slip rings . They are fastened to the shaft and rotate with it but are electrically insulated . Other alternator designs use a stationary field coil without brushes or slip rings. Here the magnetic flux of the field coil reaches the rotating magnet poles through a gap between stationary and rotating components.

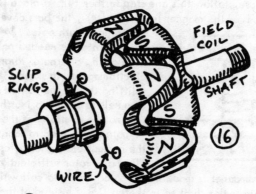

Finally, sketch (16) shows a typical rotor. Poles are marked with letters N and S , they are spaced far enough from each other to have the magnetic flux pass through the stator instead of being short circuited by flowing directly between rotor North and South poles. In the alternator, the iron core of the stator with its generating coil windings would be located directly at the magnet poles of the rotor, with just enough clearance to let the rotor spin freely.

Between the magnet poles, the wire windings of the field coil are sketched. The ends of the coil wire are passed through two holes and are connected to the slip rings. Alternators which use a needle bearing at the slip ring end of the shaft will have the plain end of the shaft as sketched here. If a ball bearing is used, its inner race will be press fitted on the shaft and the outer race will then be located directly next to the two slip rings and will usually also have the same diameter as the rings.

Note that there are a number of alternators with stationary field coils. Although they also have rotors with similar magnetic poles, the field coil will not need slip rings or brushes. Details are shown with the specific alternators which include several Delco and Marchal models.

Also note that some alternators with field brushes have one cylindrical slip ring as shown here and with a radial brush, and one disk shaped slip ring, about like a large washer, with one axial brush in its contact, the brush oriented parallel to the shaft.

And in the transition from conventional generators to alternators, some early alternators had rotors which resembled the generator rotors, with four individual magnet poles each wound with its own field coil. The outer dimensions of these early alternators also had the proportions of the longer and narrower generators.

OF ROTOR POLES AND STATOR COILS

For a general understanding of alternators, this section is not essential. But to be complete, a look at the stator is needed, at that component which contains the power generating coils and which, in contrast to the conventional generators, produces alternating current. The transition to alternators on a broad scale became possible when capable and inexpensive solid state rectifying diodes became available. And with them, the "self rectifying AC generator" made use of several phenomena related to alternating current to improve its performance and reduce its size. In this section, we will see how present alternators use three phase alternating current, as well as high frequency AC, to make conventional generators obsolete.

The stator coils or stationary power generating coils produce pulses of electricity when the magnetic poles of the rotor pass by. We have seen earlier (sketch ⑤ ⑥ ⑦) that impulses from N poles have the opposite polarity of those from S poles. Our goal is to have many coils located around a rotor with many magnet poles as in sketch ⑪ . We did not connect the coils there because we have to do some thinking first.

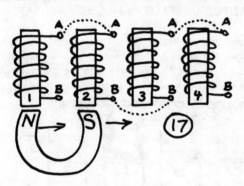

If we move the magnet in sketch ⑰ along the coils and want to connect the coils in series, so that we get highest generated voltage, we must connect as indicated by the dotted lines. That is because pulses generated, for example, in coils 1 and 2 will always have opposite polarities, plus and minus at opposite ends. To have the coils push in the same direction, or correctly add the voltage of one coil to that of the next, there are three practical ways:

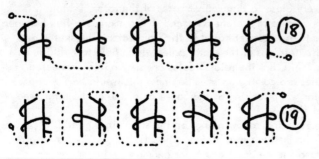

Sketch ⑱ , all coils wound in the same direction but connections change. Or sketch ⑲ , all connections are the same but winding direction changes back and forth. Or, sketch ⑳ , windings and connectiona are

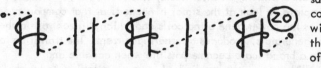

same in all coils but the windings skip the locations of the opposite magnet pole.

All these stator winding methods are actually used in alternators. The apparent waste of method ⑳ in reality is overcome by having another group of coils in the positions which were skipped . The output of the two groups of coils however must be rectified separately.

THE STATOR

Please allow me to sketch stator and rotor details in this section in a straight line, rather than in the round as they actually are. It saves space and keeps the sketches simpler which, I hope, will help them make their point more readily.

NOTE : STATOR AND ROTOR IN REALITY ARE CIRCULAR, NOT STRAIGHT AS SKETCHED IN THIS SECTION.

We have the alternator rotor, sketch ⑯ , with evenly spaced magnet poles around its edge, the poles are alternately N or S poles. To have the greatest possible magnetic flux pass through the generating coils, they are wound on a core of laminated iron which has its pole

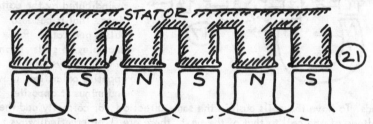

pieces extend very close to the magnet poles of the rotor, sketch ㉑ . Similar to the examples in sketches ③ and ⑬ , magnetic flux between N and S poles then is concentrated in the iron stator. The sketch also shows the small extensions at the stator poles which help to hold the coil wires in place. Note that the rotor S poles are shown interconnected while the N poles are coming up from behind : this would be the appearance of the rotor when looking at the South pole side of the rotor, see sketch ⑮ and ⑯ .

To place generating coil windings on the stator in sketch ㉑ , we can use any of the methods in sketches ⑱ , ⑲ , or ⑳ . Most often, method ⑲ appears to be practiced : for example, wire wound in right turns where a N pole is shown and left turns where S poles are .

ALTERNATING CURRENT

If the rotor in sketch ㉑ had ⑩ magnet poles, namely 5 North poles and 5 South poles, then the stator would have 10 generating coils. If

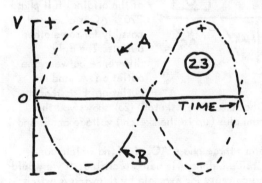

we wind them left, right, left, right, all in series, they will be about as in sketch ㉒ except, of course , located all the way around the stator and rotor. For each turn of the rotor, there will be five pulses with plus at terminal A , and five pulses with plus at terminal B . Voltage at terminal A will change back and forth from plus to minus. When A is at its highest positive voltage, B is at its highest negative voltage. Our alternator generates so called full phase alternating current or AC .

You probably have seen curves which represent voltages of AC versus time. For terminals A and B , such curves would look like this :

As voltage climbs at A to the maximum positive voltage, terminal B falls to the maximum negative voltage. The actual values depend on the number of turns in the coils, rotor speed, and strength of rotor magnetism. In 12 Volt alternators, AC voltage at open terminals, with no load connected, can easily approach 100 Volt.

How does the alternator AC compare with household 110 V AC ? The frequency of our household AC is 60 Hertz, the terminals at an outlet go through the curves in sketch ㉓ sixty times each second. The frequency of an alternator with 10 rotor magnet poles has to make only six full revolutions per second, or run at 360 RPM to generate AC of 60 Hertz (Hz). Usually, alternators are belted with pulley sizes which make alternators run twice as fast or faster than the engine. An engine operated at 2000 RPM would have its alternator run at 4000 RPM or 66.6 turns per second, generating AC of 666 Hz. As an average, the alternator frequency will be about 10 to 20 times that of household AC.

The main advantage of higher frequency is smaller size, or greater power from a given size of alternator. Military equipment often operates with 400 Hz alternating current : if you have a chance, see how much smaller motors or transformers are when compared to 60 Hz units of same horsepower or wattage.

The alternating current from the alternator of sketch ㉑ - ㉒, traced in sketch ㉓ , is called full phase. You may have heard the term split phase : it describes the kind of AC supplied by most 110 V AC outlets, for example in households. Most often, full phase AC as in sketch ㉓ , but of 220 Volt or so, is supplied by the electric company. If just one of the two wires, for example terminal A , is connected to an outlet and the other outlet terminal connected to ground (the so called neutral wire) , then the voltage between the outlet terminals can

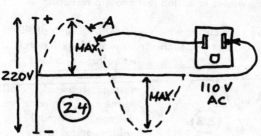

can reach a maximum of 110 V, see MAX in sketch ㉔ . The outlet carries split phase AC. The other terminal, B , of the original full phase 220 V AC is also used, possibly for some other outlets. The only difference between the outlet on A and any outlet on B is that the AC pulses do not occur at the same time : sketch ㉓ shows you that time passes between maximum plus (up in the sketch) voltage at B and maximum plus voltage at A .

There is another term : three phase AC, the kind which our alternators are generating inside before it is being rectified. If we would rectify the usual alternating current, for example by throwing a switch at the right moment, see sketch ㉕ , the result would be a chopped

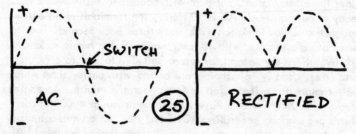

direct current as shown on the right. The AC pulses are switched and now all go in the same direction. This direct current is useful to charge batteries, it can be made into smooth DC when necessary.

THREE PHASE ALTERNATING CURRENT

We have looked at the output of alternating current (AC) from a single generating coil, for example that in sketch ㉒ , traced in sketch ㉓. If we had two coils instead, their output pulses would be either completely alike or completely opposite to each other. But in each case, we can connect the coils in parallel by choosing the correct pairs of terminals. The result would be alternating current as from a single coil. But if we had three separate generating coils, spaced evenly so that the AC pulses from each occur in a 1 - 2 - 3 - 1 - 2 - 3 fashion as in

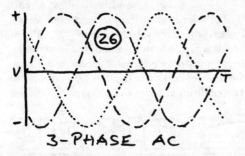

3-PHASE AC

㉖ , and then rectified the output from each coil as sketched in ㉗ , you can see that the result is much closer to smooth direct current. Even though the voltage of each coil terminal is at zero, the horizontal axis, between pulses, the rectified output of

all three coils combined , or connected to one common output terminal, does not look like the tracings in sketch ㉗ . Instead, when the voltage from the first coil or phase begins to fall, the pulse from the next coil is near and then takes over, to keep the voltage up. Then the pulse from the third coil is next, and so on. In reality, the voltage at the output terminal is

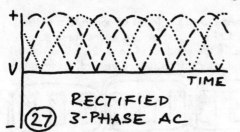

RECTIFIED
㉗ 3-PHASE AC

determined by the highest peak in effect at any moment. It looks like curve in sketch ㉘ . The voltage difference between the crests and valleys is called ripple. Ripple disappears almost entirely when the alternator is connected to a battery.

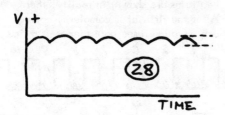

TIME

To generate three phases of alternating current, we have to modify the rotor coils. Instead of one set of coils which are connected in series as in sketch ㉒ , we need three separate sets as shown by the numbers in sketch ㉚ : the generating coils of set "1" are located at "1", an identical set of coils, just like the ones in sketch ㉒ , is located at the places on the rotor indicated by the numbers "2", and the third set at numbers "3", all three sets consisting of individual coils which are then connected in series.

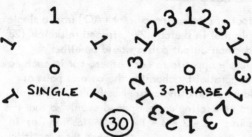

To fit all these windings on a single alternator stator is not easy. To make room for the second and third sets of coils, the iron pole pieces of the stator are made with two additional spaces : in sketch ㉛ , the

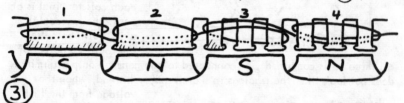

poles 1 and 2 are made for a single set of generating coils as in a single phase alternator. Coils 3 and 4 are wound three pole pieces each which have exactly the width of 1 and 2 , all coils still match the magnet poles of the rotor. If we looked upward, as from the

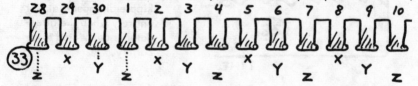

rotor on to the inner edge of the stator, we would see the windings of the first set of coils as in sketch ㉜ , done here by the "left-right-left-right" method. Two turns are shown; in reality, there are six or seven turns per coil. After the first set is complete, coils for the next set are wound similarly, around three pole pieces at a time, but over by one, sketch ㉝ . The first phase at "X", second phase at "Y", third phase at "Z", the wire turns go around the numbered pole pieces like this :

X : around 28-29-30, 1-2-3, 4-5-6, 7-8-9, ...
Y : around 29-30-1, 2-3-4, 5-6-7, 8-9-10, ...
Z : around 30-1-2, 3-4-5, 6-7-8, 9-10-11, ...

Placed side by side, the three sets of coils would look about like sketch (34) except that there are usually five, six, or seven turns in

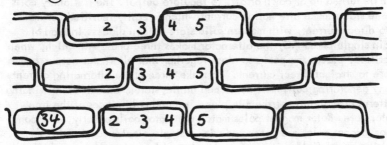

each coil, say, around poles 1-2-3 , before the wire continues to the next coil. Each of the three strings of coils, or each set or phase, has one terminal at each end. There are six ends of lacquer insulated solid copper wires altogether : the ends of the three coil "systems" which contain the power generated by the alternator, in the form of three phases of alternating current. They are connected to the rectifying diodes.

For the sake of completeness, we should have a brief look at two other "knitting patterns" different from that shown in sketch 32 . The stator wire windings could also be made as mentioned earlier and shown in sketch (20) , by winding all coils in the same direction but skipping one in-between location. In this way, coil set "X" in sketch (33) would be made by

turns around 28-29-30, passing 1, 2, 3, around 4-5-6, passing 7, 8, 9, around 10-11-12, passing 13, 14, 15, and so on until complete. All coils in the same direction, with possibly more turns in each to make up for the bypassed locations.

Finally, there is a winding method which, I am sure, was adopted to help get that much wire into such crowded space. The pattern is based

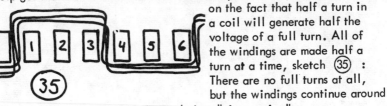

on the fact that half a turn in a coil will generate half the voltage of a full turn. All of the windings are made half a turn at a time, sketch (35) : There are no full turns at all, but the windings continue around

the stator six or seven times instead, just "zig zagging".

INTERMEDIATE SUMMARY

We looked for the difference between alternators and generators. All alternators are generators, but with a twist : what rotates is the field electromagnet while power generating coils are stationary, the stator. An electromagnet is used, rather than a permanent magnet, since it can can be turned up or down or off, to regulate output. The stationary coils of the stator make alternating current which is easily rectified, or made into direct current, with modern solid state silicon diodes. Instead of plain single phase AC, the alternator makes three phase AC which, when rectified, places the peaks so close together that alternator output comes close to straight direct current. To make three phase alternating current, many generating coils must be placed on the stator, and different winding patterns are used to get them in place, around pole pieces of the iron stator core. Rotor magnet poles match the stator coils exactly, and many rotor magnet poles are generated with a single electromagnet which consists of the field coil and two star shaped iron pieces, one making North poles and one making South poles at the edges of the rotor. Field current reaches the field coil through brushes and slip rings. Or the field coil is stationary and only the iron magnet poles rotate, in alternators without brushes.

RECTIFYING DIODES

Only after silicon rectifying diodes became available did alternators start to replace the conventional generators. A diode at one time meant a glass vacuum tube with anode, cathode, and a heating filament. Slightly more recently, selenium rectifiers came into use but were large, with low capacity and much heat output. Germanium diodes were too vulnerable, but silicon diodes were able to do the job, to rectify the alternator's AC directly within the alternator. Sketch (36) shows the diode symbol, with plus and minus signs and the names "anode" and "cathode" for the two terminals. Diodes are available in many shapes and sizes, some are shown here. They may carry a small diode symbol to identify the terminals, or may be marked with a band or ring, or may be shaped with one pointed end. Diodes for larger current often have cases (the name for the housing) with a threaded stud for heat sink mounting. Such diodes are available with the stud as anode or cathode. In alternators, diodes as the one on the bottom are most often used and are press fitted into aluminum heat sinks . This shape also is made with the knurled housing being anode or cathode.

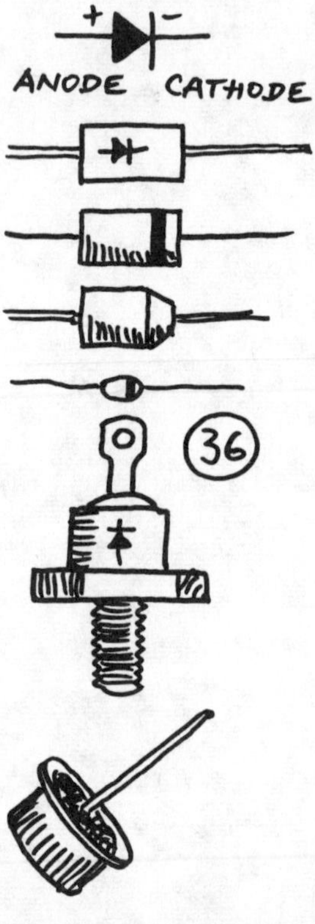

Silicon diodes have two main ratings, for the two conditions which they face : a current rating in Ampere when they are conducting in the forward direction, and a voltage rating usually called the peak invert voltage or PIV which they have to be able to hold back without becoming conductive in the reverse direction. A rectifying diode may have a rating, for examle, of 30 A, 50 PIV. The plumbing equivalent to a diode is a check valve.

To find out whether you understand how a diode works, look at the next three sketches : in (37) a diode is connected to a battery and a lamp or "light bulb". The halo around the lamp is meant to show that the lamp is on brightly. Note the direction in which the diode is connected in this circuit.

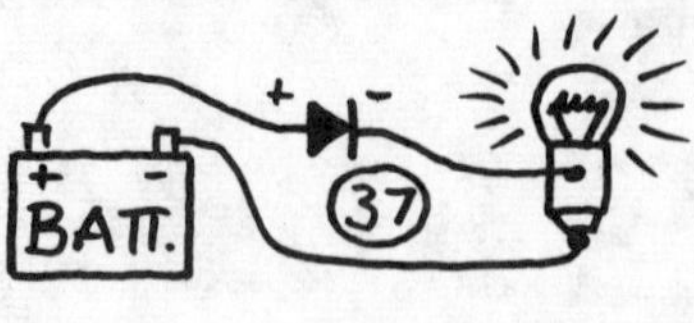

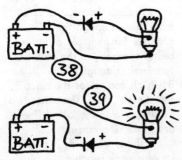

Sketch ⑱ shows the same diode in the same circuit of lamp and battery, but here connected in the opposite direction, and the lamp dark.

If you think that the bright lamp in the circuit of lamp and battery in sketch ⑲ is obvious, splendid : carry on. If there are doubts or questions, read about basic electricity, for example in "The 12 Volt Doctor's Practical Handbook", this author, Spa Creek Inc.

These sketches will also give you an idea how to test diodes with a test light and how to identify its terminals. Another test method is with a VOM (Volt Ohm Meter) in the Ohm mode.

A single diode can be used to rectify the alternating current of a generating coil. In sketch ⑳ , terminals A and B carry alternating

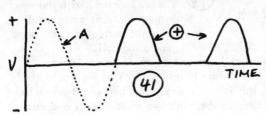

current (AC) , in quick succession, A is plus while B is minus, then B is plus while A is minus, as sketched for A with the dotted line in sketch ㉑ . But only the positive peaks are conducted through the diode which is connected to A . These positive peaks reach the plus terminal : voltage at this terminal is shown as a solid line in sketch ㉑ . Even though the single diode does not produce smooth direct current, this chopped DC is useful to charge batteries , or it can be smoothed by "filters".

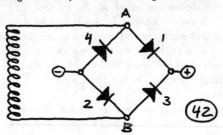

A more elegant method is to rectify with four diodes in a so called bridge circuit, or with a bridge rectifier which contains the four diodes in a single package. Sketch ㉒ shows the same generating coil with its alternating current terminals A and B which are connected to the rectifying bridge of four diodes. They are numbered : a plus peak

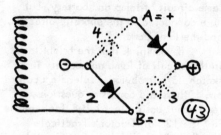

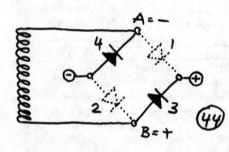

at A is conducted on by diode 1 , to reach the plus terminal, from there through the DC circuit, for example a battery being charged, to the minus terminal, through diode 2, to B which completes the circuit, see sketch ㊤ . The other two diodes, shown by dotted lines, are blockking current .

Then, when B is plus , its plus peak reaches the plus terminal through diode 3 , the DC circuit is being completed by diode 4 which connects the minus terminal to A which is minus at this moment . Sketch ㊹ shows that this time, diodes 1 and 2 are blocking .

The net effect of this diode arrangement is shown in sketch ㊹ : plus peaks at A and at B are used and rectified. In sketch ㊵ / ㊶ , peaks from B were ignored. With the new arrangement, we can expect twice the current from the same generating coil.

Now, with three generating coil sets and the three phases in the alternator , all rectified with diodes in bridge circuits, we would need a total of twelve diodes. This is rarely done, first because it would be uneconomical , but also because there are two more elegant and much simpler methods.

Sketch ㊹ on the next page shows voltages, plotted versus time, just as in the earlier sketch ㉖ . Next to it, in sketch ㊻ , the three coils of a 3-phase alternator are shown and labelled A, B, and C. The solid curve is for coil A , the dotted curve for coil B, and the broken line for coil C. Note that each curve shows the voltage at one end of its coil : if one terminal of a coil is at maximum plus voltage, or up in the graph, the other terminal of the same coil will be at the minus voltage, down in the graph, not shown but important to understand.

In this example, we will have the alternator rotor turn clockwise, as indicated in sketch ㊻ . The letters A, B, and C mark the coil terminals which are plotted in the graph.

As the rotor turns, its North and South poles pass coils A, B, C, and generate electrical pulses in a 1 - 2 - 3 - 1 - 2 - 3 fashion. Voltage at the letter-marked terminal of each coil is plotted : note the small circles

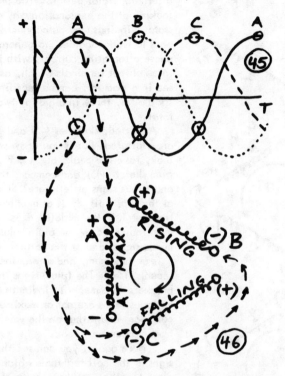

in sketch ㊺ : when voltage at coil terminal A is at maximum plus, the coil terminals B and C are near maximum minus voltage. Note the lines of arrows and see how you can find out for all six terminals whether they are plus or minus at that precise moment. When A is at maximum plus, the other end of coil B must be at maximum minus, thus the minus sign in sketch ㊻ . At the same time, the small circle below A coincides with another one around a crossing point of curves for B and C. The voltages for B and C at that instant are both minus : follow the line of arrows and mark the terminals. Terminal B is minus and rising toward zero, terminal C is minus and still falling toward its maximum minus voltage. You can now also mark the other ends of coils B and C with plus and minus signs. Interesting is that there are always two coil terminals close together in sketch ㊻ which have the same sign, plus or minus.

You can verify that : when next terminal B is at maximum plus, both terminals A and C are minus : A still falling further, C already in the process of rising toward the zero axis in sketch ㊺ .

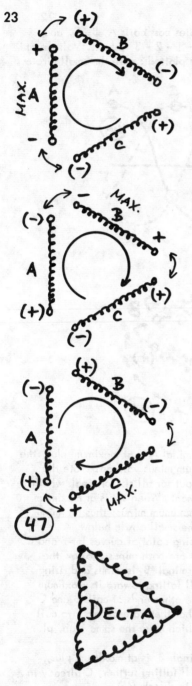

Even though you may have thrown up your hands, or worse, you have arrived in the middle of the most common of alternator stator designs. You are looking at the explanation why all three stator windings may be connected at the ends to work together, to generate three phase alternating current, with just three output terminals which, as we will see in a moment, can be rectified with six diodes, three in a group, two groups total.

Admitted, sketches (45) and (46) are cluttered. But if you know where to look, take the peaks at A , B , C , from sketch (45) and compare the plus and minus signs at left here. Starting at the top, coil A is at maximum. In the sketch in the middle, B is at maximum indicated by the plain plus and minus signs, and at the bottom, coil C is at maximum, and so on, the cycle repeats itself. The (plus) signs in brackets are meant to indicate that voltages there are not at maximum, but near, and either on the way to or from maximum or peak.

Here again, you can see that the signs at the coil terminals which are close together, at the corners of the triangle of coils match : at the coil which happens to be at maximum. And if you look closely at the other two coils, with signs in brackets : they are connected in series, just like batteries are connected in series for higher voltage. You can see, with some patience, that one coil at maximum has the other two coils contribute by combining their lesser voltage by being connected in series : and all of that if we connect the coils at the corners of the triangle. The wiring method is called DELTA because of the triangle arrangement : a "delta" wired alternator stator.

In at least one respect, the delta symbol is misleading : it may make you think that each A - B - C output cycle is with one shaft revolution. That is not the case. Look at sketch ㉛ again : if the rotor had 10 magnet poles, that is, 5 North poles and 5 South poles, we would get a series of pulses, A - B - C - A - B - C - A - B - C - A - B - C - A - B - C for just one shaft revolution. There are alternators with 14 magnet poles which will generate 7 full cycles of all three phases with each revolution.

Another comment is necessary : in the voltage graph, sketch ㊺ , voltage peaks are shown at letters A, B, and C , all on the plus side, above the zero axis, and the corresponding points in the minus region where the other two voltage curves cross, see the small circles. Omitted are just as many instances where each curve is at its lowest point, at its maximum minus voltage. At that point, the other two curves for the other two coils cross in the plus region and again, all coils cooperate. You could circle those points in the graph and, again, mark the plus or minus polarities of the separate coils, to see again how each coil contributes when they are connected to each other in "delta" fashion.

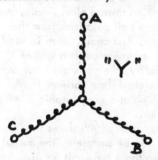

The other stator wiring method is shown here and, obviously, is called "Y" . Keep in mind that the Y symbol is only a graphic simplification which is meant to indicate that one terminal of each stator coil is connected to a common junction at the center of the Y . In reality, the stator windings are made exactly like those for the "DELTA" arrangement. The difference is how the coil terminals are interconnected.

With the Y wiring scheme, there are again three output terminals which supply 3-phase alternating current. We can label them A, B, and C again and treat them exactly like we did before. In large power generators, a wire is connected to the Y center junction and is called the neutral wire. In our alternators, the central joint exists in hiding and is usually not accessible or connected to anything else. In the review of specific alternators we will see how you can easily tell if a stator is connected "Y" or "DELTA" fashion, but for all practical purposes we can assume that the two systems are alike.

Should you wonder how the three generating coils cooperate in the "Y" wiring arrangement, look at them separately, as though they were not connected at the center of the Y , then use the voltage graph again, sketch ㊺ . Keep in mind that we had plotted the voltages at one end of each coil only. Sketch ㊽ shows the plus and minus signs for the three coils where A is at its maximum plus, B is minus and rising toward zero, C is minus and falling toward its maximum minus.

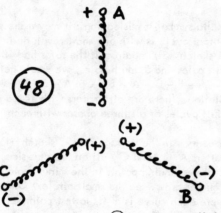

When you now imagine the three center terminals connected together, you see that both coil B and C are connected in series with coil A . At this instant, coils B and C add their generated pulses to that of coil A. All work in the same direction. The assembly happens to have one plus terminal at A and two minus terminals.

From the graph, sketch 46 , you can tell that the next plus peak occurs at B while C and A are minus. We could show the way in which the

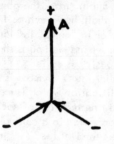

Y coils are combining their effort by arrows, sketch 49 . Long arrows mean high voltage. The arrow always pointing in the direction toward plus. Again, you can verify the coil polarities from the earlier graph. And again, keep in mind that the Y arrangement is a symbol only. In reality, the coils are made as we have sketched them earlier. Here, we are looking at a neat graphic simplification.

Finally, sketch 49 shows the peaks only. To be complete, the output pulses at the three terminals for one full phase would be; maximum voltage in this order: A+, C-, B+, A-, C+, B-, and so on. Can you see these places in the graph ? The minus peaks had not been circled.

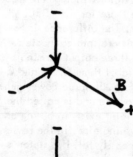

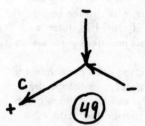

The basic reqirements are simple : we have three terminals, A, B, and C, which each produce both positive and negative pulses of alternating

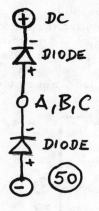

current. To use all of these, each terminal must have a conductive path to the positive as well as the negative terminal of the direct current output. That means that each AC terminal must have one diode which allows positive pulses to reach the plus DC (direct current) terminal and another diode which connects negative pulses to the negative DC output terminal. That means two diodes at terminals A, B, and C, one conducting to plus, the other conducting from minus, as in sketch ⑤⓪ . Remember that the diodes are conductive in one direction, when plus is applied to their plus (anode) terminal but block current in the other direction.

Sketches ⑤① and ⑤② show all necessary rectifying diodes for the "delta" and "Y" stators. As you can see, the rectifying circuits are identical. The sketches are simple because the three DC plus and minus

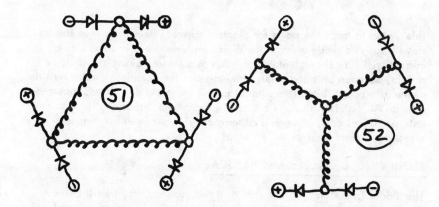

terminal are not connected to each other and to a common plus and minus output terminal. Such obviously necessary wiring often makes simple circuits more difficult to view . All you have to do here is interconnect the three plus terminals to a plus output terminals, and do the same for the three minus terminals . Several examples of these diodes are shown again, with the additional wiring, for specific models of alternators in the second section of this book.

Sketch ⑤③ shows the stator coils of an alternator in delta arrangement.
The three stator or "armature" terminals are labeled AC for alternating
current. The direct current or DC output terminals have plus and minus
signs.

   We have seen that the AC terminals in operation will have plus as
well as minus peaks as they go through their alternating current phases.
The fact that these peaks do not occur at the same time at any terminal
is the reason why each AC terminal requires its own rectifying diodes.
To conduct plus or minus pulses to the correct DC terminals, each AC
terminal needs one diode to DC plus and one diode to DC minus : use

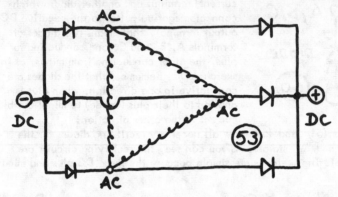

this sketch to trace the paths for electric current. Remember that current
flows through a diode only in one direction. Also keep in mind that a
current will flow through any load (such as a battery being charged, or
a light) between plus and minus terminals and the complete circuit outside
of the alternator. Note that such circuit is complete only if you can trace
from an AC terminal through a diode in the proper direction, through the
external DC circuit, through another rectifying diode in the proper
direction, and to another AC terminal.

RECTIFYING DIODES : MECHANICAL

The diodes in sketch ⑤③ are shown in two groups : note that the three
diodes near the minus terminal all have their anode in electrical contact
with the minus terminal. Similarly, the three diodes near the plus
terminal have their cathode in contact with the plus output terminal.
Since diodes produce some heat when current is flowing, they are usually
mounted on heat sinks made of metal. Such heat sink is made large
enough so that its surface can be cooled by air flow. Best thermal
contact is achieved if the three diodes are mounted directly to the heat
sink which then becomes part of the plus or minus terminal. Sometimes,
minus diodes are mounted directly to the alternator housing.

We can make a rough estimate of the amount of heat which is generated by the rectifying diodes. For example, assume that the alternator is producing 50 Ampere which are being charged into 12 Volt batteries. Silicon rectifying diodes typically will have a voltage drop of about 0.5 Volt. The 50 A flowing through the plus diodes will generate

$$0.5 \ V \ X \ 50 \ A \ = \ 25 \ W \ (Watt)$$

of heat. Since the same current also must pass the minus diodes, another 25 W of heat are generated there, for a total of 50 W . If that sounds like much to you (the heat of a 50 W light bulb or solder iron), let us compare it to the total output of the alternator :

Voltage at such relatively high current is likely 14 V or more, so that the alternator is generating

$$14 \ V \ X \ 50 \ A \ = \ 700 \ W$$

The loss at the diodes therefore is less than 10 % . Additional heat is being generated by the current in the stator windings and by the strong and rapidly changing magnetic flux in the stator and nearby metal components.

AUXILIARY DIODES

Many alternators have three additional small diodes connected between the AC stator terminals and a separate plus DC output terminal . This auxiliary terminal is often used to provide power to the field coil or to the voltage regulator. The advantage of this separate plus terminal is that its power output ceases when the alternator stops running. No switch is needed to disconnect regulator or field current, and there is no risk of electric current from batteries being wasted if any switch were left on by mistake. Power for this purpose can not be taken directly from the main plus diodes since often the battery remains connected to the plus output terminal of the alternator.

Current from the auxiliary diodes and the auxiliary terminal completes its circuit through the three main minus rectifying diodes.

Several of the alternator wiring sketches in the second part of this book show such auxiliary diodes. Their separate output terminal is often called AUX, REGULATOR, + , D+ , 61 , IND . The section on testing tells how to identify it with a meter.

ISOLATING DIODE

Another method is used to supply current to a regulator without the need for a switch. Sketch ⑤④ shows the usual three AC stator terminals and the three main plus rectifying diodes. An isolated AUX auxiliary plus

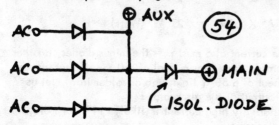

terminal is connected directly to the main diodes while the alternator's main plus output must first pass another diode : the isolating diode. Batteries may remain connected to the alternator : battery current cannot reach the auxiliary terminal which will have no output power after the alternator has stopped . A regulator may remain connected to the AUX terminal without switch and without any wasted battery power. Isolating diodes may consist of one or two individual diodes on a separate heat sink, most notably on Motorola alternators of 55A or smaller. Here, isolating diodes on a curved flat heat sink are mounted to the back housing and, of course, carry the main plus output terminal. The tests will show how to distinguish between auxiliary terminals with isolating diode or with auxiliary rectifying diodes.

ISOLATING DIODES, CHARGING DIODES, BATTERY ISOLATORS

Because of the similarity of names and components, this application of diodes should be mentioned here. Two or more diodes as in sketch ⑤⑤

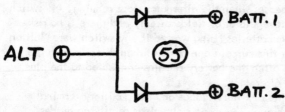

may be connected between the main alternator output terminal and the plus terminal of two or more separate batteries. With the alternator running, the two batteries in the sketch will be charged through the diodes . The lower battery by state of charge will receive greatest current. After the alternator has been stopped, batteries are isolated by the diodes : no current can flow from one battery to the other if, for example, power were taken from only one battery. The diodes have to be sufficiently large to carry the alternator output current. They are mounted on heat sinks, added to alternator-battery systems and never a part of the alternator itself.

VOLTAGE REGULATORS

Without a voltage regulator, alternator output would almost always be wrong : too low at slow speeds , or too high at high speeds, overcharging batteries, burning out lamps and equipment with excessive voltage and, possibly, destroying the rectifying diodes in the alternator.

Voltage regulators control the field current, they are always connected in series with the field coil. Voltage regulators are also connected to the alternator output terminal or to a battery plus terminal. Their function is to maintain a constant output terminal voltage by increasing or decreasing the alternator field current. The sketch shows a simplified stator and diodes, and a field coil with regulator. Field

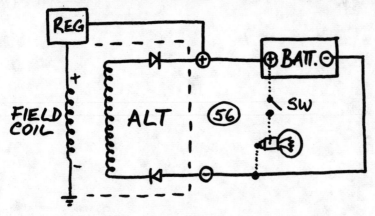

current from the plus terminal must pass the regulator which increases the magnitude of field current if voltage drops below the voltage setting which the regulator attempts to maintain. In 12 Volt systems, this voltage setting usually is 14.2 V . The sketch also shows a battery : alternators almost always operate with a battery which contributes to the voltage regulating function much like a gigantic filter capacitor. On your car, you may notice that the battery often is very small, large enough to start the engine, but too small to operate the headlights for any appreciable length of time. That is not necessary, thanks to the voltage regulator which responds with increased field current if a load, such as the lamp and switch in the sketch, are switched on. The alternator output then is increased enough so that such demands are supplied by the alternator, not the battery.

There are several types of voltage regulators in use, some of the differences are obvious, others are more subtle : there are electromechanical regulators built like relays with coils and contacts, or solid state or transistor regulators, as well as some hybrids using both techniques.

Then there are external voltage regulators mounted a distance from the alternator and connected by wires, and internal regulators located in the alternator housing. Plus a number of regulators pretending to be internal but just attached and sometimes recessed and flush with the alternator housing, usually easy to remove or replace, some as a unit with the brushes. Then there is the electrical arrangement of field coil and voltage regulator : always in series, but with regulator either at the plus side or the minus side of the field coil.

Sketch ⑤⑦ shows a relay type voltage regulator with its field coil. The relay consists if a magnet coil and a moving arm or armature with electrical contacts. The arm is held by spring tension in its normal position as sketched. The IGN ("Ignition") terminal is usually connected to battery and alternator plus terminal through the key switch, as is the

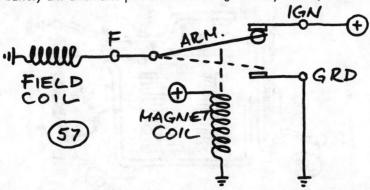

plus terminal of the magnet coil. Spring tension on the arm is made strong enough so that voltages at the magnet coil below the regulator setting will not generate enough magnetic force to move the arm. With such low voltages, full field current can flow between plus terminal, the normally closed contact, arm, F FIELD terminal, field coil, and ground, as sketched.

If voltage rises, for example due to increased alternator speed, force from the magnet coil becomes stronger until it eventually pulls the arm and opens the contact and interrupts field current. This drop in field current causes a drop in alternator output voltage which, in turn, reduces the force of the magnet coil : giving in to spring tension, the arm moves back to its normal position, closes the upper contact and reconnects full field current. Again, alternator output voltage rises and the process repeats itself : magnet coil pulls, contact opens, field current and alternator output voltage fall and magnet coil lets go of the arm again. The operation still provides smooth proportional voltage regulation because the regulator contact opens and closes very quickly, it oscillates, and field current, even though it is chopped, increases or decreases as the arm makes contact for longer or shorter times in each of these very short switching cycles. Very often, the spring tension which tends to hold the arm in its normal position can be adjusted and can be used to change the voltage setting of the regulator upward or down : increased spring tension increases the time in each switching cycle with the upper contact closed and field current connected, causing an increase of the voltage which the regulator maintains.

A similar design is shown in sketch ⑤⑧ , here with more of the mechanical details. In the center is the magnet coil : one end of its winding is connected to the steel frame which is the plus terminal. The other end is visible and shown connected to ground. The moving arm here has two contacts which are located above and below a fixed contact at A . The pivot is at the upper right and consists of a thin piece of

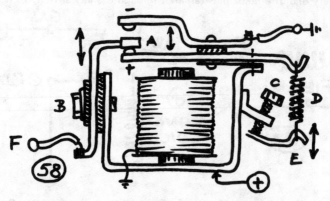

spring steel. Through the steel frame and pivot, the lower moving contact is connected to plus. The upper moving contact is insulated and connected with a wire to ground. In operation, increasing voltage lets the magnet coil attract the arm, break contact between the plus contact and fixed contact A , and makes contact between A and the minus contact. The fixed contact A is connected to the alternator field coil.

Two adjustments are shown which both influence the regulator voltage setting. A small bolt B holds the fixed contact and allows an adjustment of the air gap between magnet coil and the moving arm. If fixed contact A is moved downward, it brings the arm into closer proximity of the electromagnet, with the effect that less current through the coil will be able to attract and move the arm : this will lower the voltage setting. On the right, a coil spring D outside the pivot holds the arm in contact between plus and A . The small screw C allows the lower hook E to be moved and spring tension on the arm to be changed. Turning the screw in and moving hook E down increases coil spring tension and, as the arm oscillates, increases contact time between the moving plus contact and fixed contact A which increases the regulator voltage setting.

Often there are two relay coils and sets of contacts within the housing of a voltage regulator unit. In addition to the actual voltage regulator, there often is a field relay which may be connected to an R or RELAY terminal on the alternator, usually connected to the stator windings. This relay closes its contact when the alternator begins to generate alternating current. It connects the regulator plus terminal directly to battery and alternator plus terminals after the engine has been started. It disconnects the regulator after the engine has been stopped and prevents drained batteries. Until the field relay closes contacts, the initial field current is supplied from the ignition key switch. A typical arrangement is shown in sketch 59 .

The voltage regulator coil is at the right, with two contacts being attracted by the coil, with fixed contact between them, connected to the field coil. The field relay is at left. Initially, voltage is applied

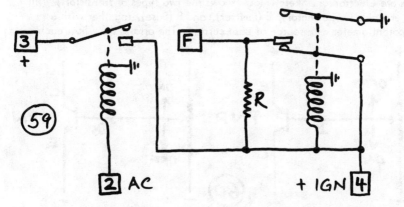

from the ignition key switch to terminal 4 (typical Delco-Remy voltage regulator) and allowing minimal field current to flow through a resistor R . Then, as the alternator turns at sufficient speed, alternating current from stator to terminal 2 causes the relay contact to close, making a direct connection from battery plus terminal to terminal 3 and to coil and contact of the voltage regulator. At that point, power from terminal 4 is no longer needed. After the alternator has stopped, the field relay contacts open again and prevent continued flow of field current.

The usual charge indicator light or "idiot light" is connected in the wire between ignition key and terminal 4 . It lights only while current flows between key switch and terminal 4 and goes out when the relay connects terminal 3 : at that point, plus voltage reach the light both from the key switch and from terminal 3 . Current stops to flow through the light since both of its terminals are at the same positive voltage.

Regulators with three relay units were in use with generators. A third
relay was needed to disconnect the output terminal from the battery at
low speeds and when the generator was not running. This output relay is
not needed with alternators since the rectifying diodes prevent current
in reverse when the alternator is off. Still, some such voltage regulators
with a third output relay have been used with some alternators during a
transition period.

To discuss solid state or transistor regulators, some very brief
look at transistors is needed and at their way of operation. Transistors
have three terminals : an inlet and outlet and a terminal which is called
the base and which controls the transistor's conductivity. With the base,
transistors can be turned on and off and change their resistance. The
two types are called NPN and PNP transistors, N and P stand for Positive
and Negative and describe the junctions, look it up in a text on solid
state electronics. Sketch (60) shows the two types of transistors, with
terminals C (Collector), E (Emitter), and B (Base), together with a
potentiometer as a source of base current. The arrows show how each

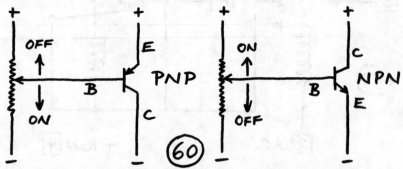

transistor can be turned on or off, or made more or less conductive. If,
for example, the wiper of the potentiometer (variable resistor) on the
NPN transistor wre moved up, closer to the plus terminal, more base
current would flow which makes the transistor more conductive, letting
greater current flow between emitter and collector.

To handle typical alternator field current which amounts to
several Ampere, a power transistor is needed which in turn needs larger
base currents to be fully turned on. Usually therefore, a second transistor
is used to control base current of the power transistor.

Finally, an element usually used in solid state voltage regulators is a Zener diode which becomes conductive in reverse (plus on
cathode, minus on anode) at a specific voltage, for example 10 Volt,
and which is used in the voltage sensing circuit, improving the
potentiometers in sketch (60) . The symbol for a Zener diode is shown
at left. Other, similar symbols have also been used,
all are modifications of the diode symbol shown earlier.

The voltage regulator in sketch ⑥1 has a power transistor A which is capable to handle the needed current for the field coil. Since such power transistors usually require relatively large base currents to be turned on, a small transistor B is connected in a so called Darlington circuit to

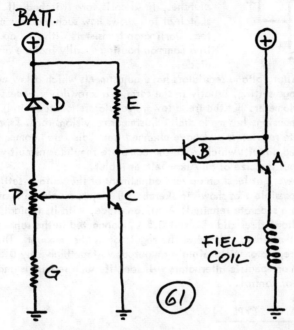

BATT.

FIELD COIL

⑥1

switch base current for the power transistor. Much less base current is needed for transistor B : that base current is supplied through resistor E. At low battery voltages, Zener diode D does not conduct and transistor C is off. As battery voltage rises, diode D begins to conduct and through potentiometer P , base current turns transistor C on : it conducts current through E to ground, shorts the base of B to ground which turns off B and A , and interrupts field current. Similar to the vibrating contacts in the mechanical regulators, this transistor regulator switches back and forth between more and less conductive states of the transistors.

There are two plus terminals : the one at the right often is supplied by auxiliary diodes, relay, key switch, oil or fuel pressure switch, or by alternator output with isolating diode. Voltage at this terminal often is different from battery voltage. The plus terminal at left senses battery voltage and often remains connected permanently to the battery since only very little current is used by this terminal.

A large number of variations of this circuit is possible. A few additional examples are among the specific alternators in the second half of the book. Not shown here, but necessary, are some protective

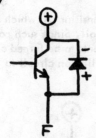

components. Most important is a diode which will allow reverse voltage spikes to bypass the power transistor instead of ruining it. Such spikes are generated when inductive loads, such as coils in solenoids, relays, compressor clutches, field coils, are switched off. The sketch at left shows how such diode is connected. Darlington transistors with "A" and "B" in a common housing usually include a reverse diode.

Some transistor voltage regulators have adjustments which allow changing of the voltage setting, usually in the form of a screwdriver accessible trim potentiometer. But the trend toward regulators located within the alternator housings has made such adjustment provisions rare. Especially as solid state regulators also have changed from "discrete" components to integrated circuits which make the complete regulator circuit with housing about the size of an Alka-Seltzer tablet.

However, at least an upward adjustment of the voltage setting is often still possible : as shown in sketch ⑥1 , system voltage is often sensed with a separate terminal. A silicon diode, with its typical forward voltage threshold of about 0.5 V, connected in the sense wire, will lower the sensed voltage at the regulator by that amount . The result is that the regulator will maintain an output voltage higher by 0.5 V . The section on specific alternators will identify such terminals and some of methods of control.

TYPE P AND TYPE N

Regulators control field current by being connected in series with the alternator field coil. There are two possible arrangements, both are in

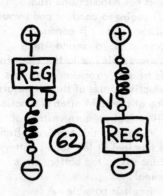

use. The voltage regulator may be on the positive side of the field coil, between a source of positive voltage and the positive field coil terminal, or the regulator may be on the negative side of the field coil, between the negative field coil terminal and negative system terminal which most often is ground. We will call the first arrangement type P for Positive, the second arrangement type N , as shown in sketch ⑥2 . Do not confuse with positive ground (rare) or negative ground (most common) wiring systems. The two are not related.

With the more usual negative ground system, and with brushes at the terminals of the field coil, alternators with type P arrangement, with the regulator on the plus side of the field coil, one brush will be grounded. In contrast, type N alternators will have none of the brushes connected directly to ground, see sketch ⑥②.

In general, electromechanical or relay type regulators will be external, located at a distance from the alternator and connected by wires to the alternator, and will be of type P .

External solid state or transistor regulators often replace a mechanical version, have housings and terminals like the mechanical version and operate as type P . But more recent external solid state regulators may be of type N . If you need to know, a test or close inspection will tell the difference.

Internal voltage regulators, including those which are attached, inserted or somehow a part of the alternator itself are most often a type N , with the notable exception of the smaller Motorola alternators with attached regulator.

In the description of alternators and their regulators, we will use these terms :

POSITIVE GROUND : rare, has battery plus terminal connected to engine block or starter housing.

NEGATIVE GROUND : most common, has battery minus terminal connected to engine block or starter housing . Alternator minus terminal may be connected to alternator housing, grounded through metal bracket.

ISOLATED GROUND : neither plus nor minus battery terminal is permanently connected to ground or starter housing or engine block. Both plus and minus starter wires (cables) are switched by solenoid for engine starting. Sometimes, only during starting, battery minus becomes engine ground.

TYPE P ALTERNATOR/REGULATOR : external or attached voltage regulator is connected to plus field coil terminal or plus brush. Minus brush usually grounded or to minus.

TYPE N ALTERNATOR/REGULATOR : voltage regulator is connected between minus field coil terminal and ground or minus. Plus brush or field terminal is connected to auxiliary plus terminal or system plus. Minus brush or field coil terminal not connected to ground or minus but to regulator.

EXTERNAL VOLTAGE REGULATOR : separate unit connected to the alternator by one or more wires.

INTERNAL VOLTAGE REGULATOR : located within the alternator back housing, or attached to the alternator.

ELECTROMECHANICAL VOLTAGE REGULATOR : relay type with coil and contacts, always external.

SOLID STATE VOLTAGE REGULATOR : has no moving contacts, made from discrete transistors and components, or consisting of integrated circuit(s).

Many alternators take the power for their field current from their own
generated output. They are mainly the alternators with isolating diode or
with auxiliary diodes. Both designs use the diodes to make external relays
unnecessary. They can then use very compact solid state regulators which
find space within the alternator. When such alternator is not running, the
isolating diode, for example, prevents current from the battery to be
wasted on field current. The battery can remain connected to the alternator output terminal at all times. However, a slight drawback of this
design is apparent immediately after the alternator starts to run : there is
no field current because there is no power being generated, and that is
because there is no field current. One has to come first, and from an
outside source : the battery. The process is called excitation.

Excitation current is usually taken from an ignition switch or engine
key switch and is supplied to the field coil through a resistor. Often, a
charging light, alternator pilot light or idiot light is used and then
contributes to the excitation current, as in sketch ⑥③ . Once the alternator is in full normal operation, regulator and field coil get their power

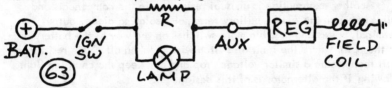

from the auxiliary (AUX) terminal. But directly after startup, excitation
current from the ignition switch (IGN SW) through resistor R and the
indicator light LAMP must reach the AUX terminal to start the generating
process. It takes less than a second to start, and the needed current is
less than one amp. Then, the AUX terminal carries output voltage and
the lamp finds itself with about battery voltage at both sides : it stops to
light. The resistor is used so that the alternator is being excited even if
the lamp burns out. The resistor is necessary to prevent high battery
charging current to flow through thin wires from AUX terminal through
the ignition switch to the battery. The resistor is usually between 50 and
150 Ohm. Note that regulator and field coil are of the type P in this
sketch.

One peculiarity with charge indicator lights is that sometimes they
will not comletely extinguish even though the alternator performs quite
normally. One explanation is shown in sketch ⑥④ where you see same
excitation circuit with ignition switch, resistor R, charge indicator
light, connected to the AUX terminal of the alternator. Once the
generating process has been cycled into operation, alternating current
AC is being rectified : only the three positive rectifying diodes are

shown which connect to the auxiliary terminal, as does the light. On the way to the battery, alternator output current must also pass the isolating diode which electrically is between AUX terminal and the alternator's OUTPUT terminal. And this diode, or a pair in parallel, creates a small

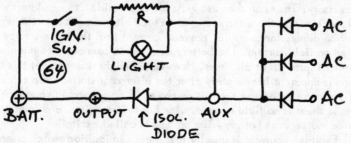

voltage drop, about one volt or less : the AUX terminal and the right side of the lamp will be about one volt higher than the OUTPUT terminal and the left side of the lamp. While that will not start a cold lamp to glow, it may keep one glowing which just had been at full brightness.

Another explanation is unusual resistance in the components and wires between the AUX auxiliary terminal, isolating diode, output terminal, wires and possible main switches on the way to the battery or to the point where the ignition switch wire is taken off. Such resistance will then create a similar voltage drop and can keep the charging light glowing if the alternator is of this design.

The most practical cure, if no other corrective steps are necessary, is to switch to a lamp ("light bulb") with slightly higher design voltage or slightly higher Watt rating.

A diode can also be used to supply excitation current, shown in sketch ⑥⑤ . The diode will apply almost full battery voltage to the auxiliary terminal and will tend to create much greater excitation currents than resistor and light , neither good nor bad. However, such diode prevents all feedback to the ignition switch, an advantage when

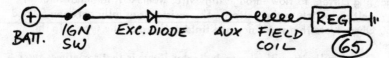

certain accessories are powered from the switch : for example, fuel solenoid valves may close more immediately when the switch is being opened .

Note that field coil and regulator in sketch ⑥⑤ are the type N wiring arrangement, with the regulator between field coil and ground.

BATTERY

IMPORTANT : Alternators are designed to operate in conjunction with a battery . They must be connected to a battery while running. Interrupting the running alternator from the battery , even for only a fraction of a second, can have the alternator output voltage rise high enough to cause one or more of the rectifying diodes to fail.

Alternator and battery cooperate with each other. The battery usually supplies power to start the engine and excite the alternator. The alternator then recharges the battery . Starting batteries have to supply very high current to the starter motor, but usually only for a very short time, so that the needed Ampere hours are small and the battery itself can be relatively small. Still, relatively high currents can be drawn from the alternator-battery combination indefinitely, as long as the alternator is running at sufficient speed and such current is within the alternator's capacity.

For example, a large engine in a car may need 200 Ampere for its starting motor, supplied by a 12 V battery. If the engine starts after 10 seconds of cranking, the Ampere hours taken from the battery are :

$$200 \text{ A} \quad \text{X} \quad (\ 10 \ / \ 60 \ / \ 60 \ ) \text{ hours} \quad = \quad 0.56 \text{ Ampere hours,}$$

which is less than one hundredth of the total storage capacity of a typical 60 Ampere hour battery. The battery will be recharged quickly after starting and will essentially be fully charged at all times.

If then electrical equipment is being switched on, drawing, for example, 30 Ampere, the voltage regulator instantly increases the alternator output current by 30 Ampere so that the battery remains unaffected . In fact, as long as the capacity of the alternator is greater than 30 A and runs fast enough, it will supply the 30 A draw and at the same time continue to charge the battery. That is because the voltage regulator usually is adjusted to maintain a voltage at the alternator output terminal which is slightly higher than the voltage which the battery can ever achieve, even when fully charged.

The alternator output voltage is usually maintained by the voltage regulator at

14.0 V - 14.4 V for 12 Volt systems ,
28.0 V - 28.8 V for 24 Volt systems , and
37.4 V - 38.4 V for 32 Volt systems.

The 12 V battery typically shows a voltage of 13.2 to 13.8 when it is completely charged. Depending on electricity use, including current drawn at idle speeds or while the engine is off, the voltage setting of the alternator is a compromise which may mildly overcharge the battery,

43

or not charge it quite enough. The first case is noticeable when water in the cells of the battery has to be replenished frequently. Undercharged batteries will not reach a voltage typical for full charge, and the smaller amount of stored electricity, in Ampere hours, will make itself known when current must be drawn from the battery *.

The connection to a single battery can be made directly, as shown at top in sketch (66), by a wire heavy enough to carry maximum alternator output, usually a size 10 or 8 AWG, stranded copper, but sometimes consisting of two parallel wires of smaller cross section. The

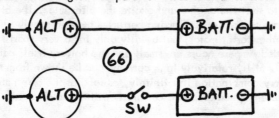

wire may be permanently connected to the alternator output terminal. No current can flow in reverse : the rectifying diodes prevent that. Sometimes, a switch is used as shown at the lower sketch , such switch is only useful or necessary if electrical equipment must be switched and if another wire between switch and battery is impractical. Such main switch may be used to disconnect battery from starter solenoid. There is some risk that the switch may be accidentally opened while the alternator is operating. This can destroy one or more of the rectifying diodes.

A main switch is often used when there are two or more separate batteries connected to an alternator. Such switch, top in sketch (67), is a single pole – double throw (SPDT) switch which should be a "make before break" type : when switching from "1" to "2", it makes the connection to terminal 2 before breaking the connection to terminal 1. The switch position which has all three terminals interconnected, usually named "ALL" or "BOTH" should be used before starting engine and

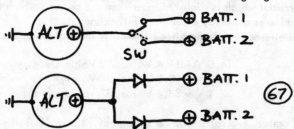

alternator, to connect all batteries to the alternator before starting, and after charging them with the alternator, select the battery to be used.

and separate the other one as standby. Such switching can be made automatic with so called isolating diodes, splitter diodes, charging diodes, or battery isolators, shown at the bottom in sketch 67 and again in sketch (68) . Such devices connect a diode between alternator output terminal and the plus terminal of a single battery. Charging current can reach the battery but battery current cannot exit the battery, except if you choose so, by switch setting. Each separate battery needs its charging diode. The diode must have a current rating in Ampere to match or exceed the anticipated maximum charging current. Such diodes are mounted on "heat sinks" of finned aluminum since some heat is being generated when current is flowing. Note that a "separate battery" may consist of two or more batteries which are connected in parallel, to make a larger battery bank which acts as a single battery of larger storage capacity. Details can be found in books on electricity.

One practical way to connect charging diodes where there is a battery main switch or selector switch is shown in sketch (68) : since sufficiently heavy wiring already is in place between the switch and the alternator and the batteries, diodes can be connected directly to the

switch terminals as shown, and the diodes possibly located behind the panel which carries the switch.

The charging diodes or isolating diodes (same name, but different from the isolating diode used in some alternators) cause a small voltage step or threshold when current is flowing. The difference between anode and cathode voltage is about 0.6 V for all silicon diodes regardless of size.

Example : if a charging current of 30 Ampere is flowing through a diode, the generated heat will be about 30 A X 0.6 V = 18 W (Watt) .

The small voltage drop at charging diodes can be confusing to the operation of voltage regulators : if battery voltage is sensed by a wire connected "upstream" of that diode, the voltage regulator will sense a voltage 0.6 V higher than the actual battery voltage. Since the regulator maintains the alternator output terminal voltage, usually at 14.2 V, a voltage of 0.6 V less reaches the battery. Better is to connect the voltage regulator "downstream" of the charging diode or directly to the corresponding battery terminal. Since that however may connect the regulator to a full battery where another empty battery must also be charged, a simple trick can be used to compensate for the voltage drop across charging diodes or splitters.

Sketch ⑥⑨ shows an alternator connected through charging diodes to two batteries. To compensate for the voltage drop at the charging diodes, another diode (arrow !) is connected in the plus sensing wire of the

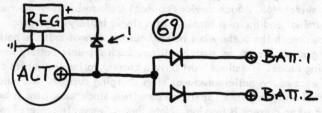

voltage regulator. This diode can be much smaller in current rating than the charging diodes but will have a very similar voltage drop or threshold which is independent of the amount of current. The voltage at the regulator will be 0.6 V lower than that of the alternator output terminal, or about the average of the two batteries, as long as some charging current is flowing.

With external voltage regulators, this compensating diode will be easy to install : look up the brand of regulator and see what letters or numbers are used to label the terminals. A suitable diode is the type

1N5400 or an equivalent, rated 3 Ampere. Its cathode will be pointed or marked with a band, see sketch ㊱ . Even simpler is the case of mechanical regulators which may have a voltage adjustment screw, or which otherwise are adjusted by bending, with suitable pliers, the spring support arm, see sketch 58 . Increased spring tension usually causes higher alternator output terminal voltage. A voltmeter is essential to make proper adjustments : 14.0 to 14.4 V at the terminals of a 12 V battery after several hours of running time, little loss of water from the batteries. Read about battery charging and battery maintenance .

Alternators with attached solid state voltage regulators or with internal regulators often do not have a separate battery sensing wire or terminal : look up the specific alternator or a similar model in the next section of this book. Some alternators make the exception : Motorola alternators with attached regulators have sense terminals or the single regulator plus wire (red) is accessible at the outside, and many Delco-Remy alternators with internal voltage regulator have two lug terminals marked "1" and "2" . Terminal 2 senses battery voltage.

---

* more on batteries, battery charging, switches, diodes, wiring, trouble shooting in "The 12 Volt Doctor's Practical Handbook.. " Edgar Beyn, 3rd edition 1983 , Spa Creek Inc. Annapolis MD .

Wiring diagrams are most useful if they clearly show how the components of a circuit are connected to each other. To explain a particular function, a wiring scetch will only show the components which are significant and otherwise only show how the connections to the rest of the whole system are made. In other words, to explain voltage regulators, only regulator and field coil with connections to plus and minus must be shown, perhaps with ignition switch, charge light, and the battery plus terminal. This, hopefully, will keep the sketches simple and understandable.

  All wires or other metal conductors are shown as solid lines. If two wires cross each other without being connected to each other, they will be shown as at A . Joints of two , three, or more electrically connected wires or other conductors are shown with a dot as at B and C . A zigzag line indicates a resistor while a row of loops mean a coil, as in a relay, solenoid, field coil, generating coil. A capacitor is shown by the two parallel plates. If it is an electrolytic type, a + sign will show polarity. The symbol for "ground" is shown : most often, it will be identical with the minus pole of the system.

  A case or housing is shown by a broken line, to indicate which components are located within. If the housing is metal, it may be connected to ground or serve as ground, as shown here by the connected ground symbol. The circle with diagonal cross shows a lamp with its two terminals. The switch symbol shows a single pole - single throw switch. Symbols for other types of switches will be obvious. Next, a plus terminal shows a resistor which is then further connected to components which are not shown : text will explain, or one of the abbreviations may tell where the arrow is eventually connected.

  Many of the abbreviations are shown here : from regulator to battery, alternator, Ampere, Volt, Watt, Ohm, resistor, ignition, alternating current, stator, field, ground, and switch. Letters N and P will refer to field-and-regulator arrangements of type "N" or type "P" , as used in this book. This designation of alternator types is not in general use.

#10 A

B

C

R

+

GRD

CASE

LAMP

SW

REG BATT.
ALT A
V W Ω
R IGN
AC STA
F GRD
SW N P

+ ‑
F
FIELD
COIL

N.O.

COIL

N.C.

COIL

R
Ω
OHM

SW.

CONNECTED

ISOLATED

GRD

While we are in the middle of it, symbols in the sketches on the following pages allow us to leave out the clutter of repeated explanations . Symbols for wires, coils, resistors, contacts, let the sketch show more clearly what is the point. Such symbols are used for field coil, at left, with + and – signs which let you see if it is a type "P" or "N" regulator or alternator. The coil symbol is also used with relays : see the ones with N.O. and N.C. contacts. The normally open (N.O.) is being pulled closed, making contact, when the coil is energised. The other, with normally closed (N.C.) contact opens or disconnects when the relay coil becomes magnetic with current and pulls the contact arm.

Note the different symbol for a resistor which is a zigzag line, often labeled R, with values in Ohm.

The switch SW in most voltage regulator sketches is the ignition switch, sometimes an oil or fuel pressure switch, usually with other funclions (such as ignition) not shown in these sketches.

Wires or other metal conductors are shown as solid lines. Where such lines cross each other, they make electrical contact only if there is a black dot . Otherwise, they cross while remaining electrically isolated from each other : see the sketches here.

The plus (+) symbol is used for several different positive terminals including the actual battery plus terminal, the plus or more positive end of the field coil, ot the plus auxiliary or main output terminal of an alternator. The list on the following page explains.

The symbol for ground, GRD, is often used to avoid tracing wiring to battery minus. It means "minus" in negative ground systems and isolated ground systems. It does not apply to positive ground systems which are not covered in this book.

If a regulator had failed altogether, the effect would be noticeable
very quickly : alternator output would stop, and voltage would fall as
electricity is drawn from the battery alone. Or voltage would briefly
rise before damaging the alternator.

Not quite so obvious is a regulator which just performs a bit out
of its expected range. Only the symptoms may be noticed : batteries
which are incompletely charged, or which need water added to the cells
often. Testing such regulator is still relatively easy. First, the most
direct and obvious :

TEST : VOLTAGE REGULATOR IN OPERATION

In a car, you can test the voltage regulator while you have to stop at
a red light. With the engine at slowest idle, notice the rate at which
the turn signal flashes, or listen to it click. Or note the relative
brightness of the headlights at night, or their yellow or more white
color reflected from some car ahead of you. Now accelerate the engine
and note any changes : if the turn signal clicks at a faster rate, or lights
become more white, less yellow in color, voltage has increased. You
could now race the engine to make sure that there is no further increase
in rate or brightness. Not necessary, and probably the light up there has
turned green and you are on your way again.

This test can be more refined with the use of a voltmeter. At very
low speed, the regulator may call for more alternator output than is
possible at such speed. Voltage is then below the setting of the voltage

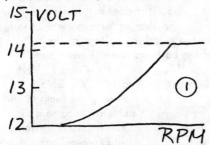

regulator, below that voltage
which the regulator attempts to
maintain. At this stage, the
voltmeter, connected to battery
posts or other place of the system,
should show the battery voltage.
If you now increase engine
speed, voltage should gradually
increase, as shown in the sketch.
The rate of increase, and the
alternator speed are not specified. Voltage will climb more rapidly if
the alternator is big, the battery relatively small, and speed high. But
much more important is that once voltage reaches about 14.2 V in a
12 Volt system, or about 28.5 V in 24 V systems, it will not rise any
further . That is because the regulator should not let it rise further.

TEST REGULATOR SEPARATELY

We want to test whether the voltage regulator responds to voltage changes. One possible voltage source is shown in sketch ②. It consists of a battery and a battery charger. The battery charger is large enough to be able to overcharge the battery : that is precisely the condition, read "voltage", where we want the voltage regulator to switch off.

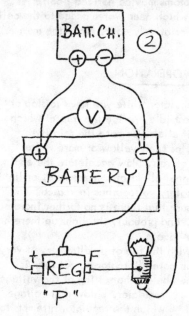

Best is a plain, unregulated or non-automatic battery charger rated, for example, 15 Amp., and a battery , not too large, which is already nearly fully charged. A voltmeter is needed to show the voltage at which the regulator switches.

In place of the alternator field coil we use a lamp ("light bulb") : you can easily solder wires directly to most lamps. Hook to regulator and battery, and connect the other regulator terminals as shown. Note that we are dealing with a type P regulator, such as the great majority of external voltage regulators.

At first, the lamp will light up. If it does not, disconnect the charger for a moment. The battery voltage should be lower than the switching voltage of the regulator. Now let the charger feed the battery. The voltmeter should show slowly increasing values, such as 13.5 to 14 Volt with a 12 Volt battery. Then, as we reach values between 14.2 to 14.6 V (12 Volt

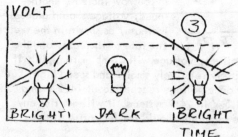

systems), the lamp should suddenly become dark as the regulator switches "field current" off.

Switch off the battery charger and watch the meter : as voltage falls, the lamp should suddenly become bright again. The voltage curve is shown in sketch ③ , together with the switching voltage (the broken line) and phases where the lamp is bright or dark.

To test a type N regulator, we use the same "variable voltage" source, namely the battery and charger, and connect the regulator to the lamp,

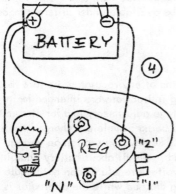

pretending that the lamp is the field coil. Sketch ④ shows the outline of a Delco internal solid state regulator. Spade lug terminal "2" must be connected to +BATT, lamp and minus wire as shown, to the metal inserts imbedded in the plastic regulator housing. Increase battery voltage by starting the charger. The lamp should become dark when battery voltage reaches 14.2 to 14.4 V for 12 Volt regulators.

VOLTAGE REGULATOR AND BATTERY CHARGING

The voltage regulator setting, that is the voltage which it maintains at the alternator output terminal, is always slightly higher than the highest voltage which the battery, standing by itself, can reach. That means, the battery is going to be overcharged slightly after it has reached full charge. Before it reaches full charge however, the charging rate depends on the voltage regulator setting and may at times be too slow. As you can see, the regulator setting is a compromise : high enough to create a large enough battery charging current before the battery reaches full charge, yet low enough to minimize the effects of overcharging, after the battery has reached full charge.

The recommendations of alternator manufacturers are toward a voltage regulator setting which during average use of the electrical system causes some noticeable consumption of water in the cells of the battery, meaning that the batteries are being lightly overcharged. This then makes certain that batteries from time to time during their normal use reach full charge. Which in turn is important to the life of the battery : if not fully charged from time to time, the unused portion of the battery's storage capacity is being lost, the battery is getting smaller, its Amper hour rating is decreasing. Since batteries age and eventually fail by gradual loss of storage capacity, incomplete recharging will contribute to this process and reduce the useful life of the battery.

We have seen how the voltage setting of mechanical, relay type voltage regulators can be changed, namely by changing spring tension at the armature of such voltage sensitive relay. Although some solid state regulators have provisions for voltage adjustments, usually in the form of screwdriver adjustments of small potentiometers or resistors,

51

the majority do not. In most applications, such adjustment is not needed.
Solid state regulators are usually manufactured with a range of voltage
settings and the same regulator may be available under different model
numbers with different voltages.

VOLTAGE REGULATOR SETTING

Before attempting to change the setting of any regulator, be sure that
the reasoning is sound. The following instructions are intended mainly
for solid state regulators without voltage adjustment, and for circumstan-
ces where batteries are obviously not being completely charged even
though an alternator is in operation. Review the section on voltage
regulators and battery charging. Read in detail about battery charging
and, especially, be aware that the voltage regulator can not handle
charging of batteries which are being drained while the alternator is
not running. In such cases, faster recharging results but is invariably
leading to overcharging unless the alternator is being stopped in time.

      All voltage regulators respond to an increase of battery
voltage with a decrease in field current. It is relatively easy to reduce
the battery voltage before it reaches the regulator. It is impractical to
increase the battery voltage. We will limit efforts to the practical and
discuss how to fool the regulator with a manipulated lower battery
voltage which will cause the voltage regulator to attempt to maintain
an increased alternator output voltage.

      Although a resistor in the wire between regulator and
+BATT will have a voltage drop, a resistor in this application will give
poor results because the voltage drop will vary with current. The true

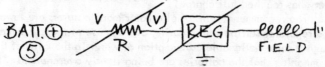

battery voltage V , sketch ⑤ , will drop to an uncontrolled voltage
(V) which will fall as the regulator increases field current. Rather, a
diode is used as in sketch ⑥ . Silicon diodes typically have a voltage
drop of 0.6 V which is constant within a wide range of currents. Here,

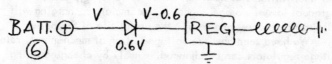

the regulator responds to a voltage which is 0.6 V below the actual
battery voltage. The regulator attempts to maintain an alternator output
voltage 0.6 V higher than it did without the diode.

With 3 - terminal regulators as in sketch ⑥ , the diode must be able to
carry full field current . And if the regulator voltage is to be increased
by more than 0.6 V, two or more diodes are used in series, each
contributing its threshold voltage and lifting the alternator output voltage
by 0.6 V. Also, each must have a current rating in Ampere equal to, or
greater than maximum field current .

    One of the most common type N regulators is shown in sketch ⑦ .
Alternator output voltage is being increased by about 0.6 V when a
silicon diode is connected between +BATT and spade lug terminal "2"
as shown, with the cathode toward the regulator. In this case , as with
most other type N regulators, the supply of plus field current comes from
a diode trio or auxiliary terminal and is not supplied through the sensing
terminal. Therefore, the diode current rating is not as critical as it is
with the type P regulators. However, should the diode fail by becoming
nonconductive, or should the connection break, the alternator will
increase its output to near maximum.

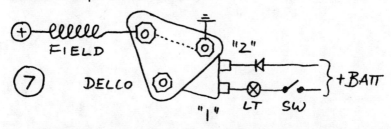

The sketch also shows a charge indicator light LT with switch SW, the
normal method to excite the alternator through terminal "1" .

The main reason to lift alternator output voltage with a diode at the
voltage regulator is to overcome the effect of charging diodes, also
called splitter diodes or isolators which are connected between alternator
output terminal and two or more separate batteries which must be charged
from one alternator but must be kept isolated from each other. Since
such larger diodes introduce the same 0.6 V threshold between alternator
and batteries, a regulator often measures a voltage which is 0.6 V higher
than actual battery voltage.

Under certain conditions, it can become difficult to recharge batteries with an alternator if electricity is being drained from the batteries first, while an alternator is not in operation at the same time. Subsequent recharging then requires long alternator running time which may become objectionable. In such cases only, manual alternator controls are used to, temporarily, control alternator output current by hand, rather than alternator output voltage by voltage regulator.

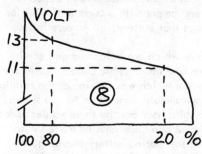

The background : the voltage of lead – acid batteries is not constant. Rather, it depends on the state of charge of the battery. For a 12 V battery, the voltage, without any current flowing, is over 13 when the battery is nearly fully charged, and below 11 V when the battery is nearly empty. In sketch ⑧, the approximate shape of the curve is shown against a scale of percent of full charge. Such curve applies to batteries of all sizes.

To charge the battery, a current must be made to flow in the opposite direction of currents which flow when battery electricity is being used. To make such charging current flow, the alternator must apply a voltage to the battery which is higher than the voltages in sketch ⑧ .The excess voltage beyond the battery's standby voltage must drive the chemical reactions which take place at the battery plates during charging, and must cause charging current to flow according to Ohm's Law : current in Ampere is determined by the excess voltage and the resistance of the circuit. Although the internal resistance of batteries is very low, the wires to and from the battery, the rectifying diodes and stator coil windings in the alternator are all a part of this circuit.

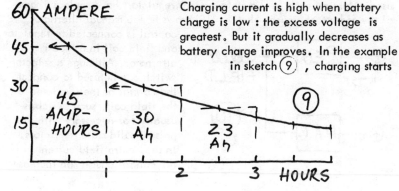

Charging current is high when battery charge is low : the excess voltage is greatest. But it gradually decreases as battery charge improves. In the example in sketch ⑨ , charging starts at 60 A (Ampere) and gradually falls. At the end of the first hour, charging current has decreased to about 40 A, and so on. To estimate if such a rate is adequate to charge a given battery, we must know the capacity of the battery which is given in Ampere hours (Ah) and its state of charge or "condition".

For example, a battery of 120 Ampere hour capacity or size, half charged or at 50 %, has room for 60 Ah (Ampere hours) and could be charged with 15 Ampere for 4 hours to reach full charge.

Another example : a battery of undetermined size or capacity has been used to power a piece of equipment with a current of 10 A for a period of 8 hours. To fully recharge that battery, 80 Ampere hours must be charged.

In sketch ⑨, the Ampere hours which are being charged can be estimated easily. For each hour, we find the average current during that hour. That is approximately the current which was flowing at the middle of that hour. For each hour, the approximate amounts in Ah are shown. The total charged at the end of the third hour are the three values added together, or 98 Ah . A similar estimate can sometimes be made by just having an occasional look at an ammeter during battery charging. You should make such estimate during charging, and an estimate of Ampere hours consumed from the battery, before considering the use of a manual alternator control.

The example in sketch ⑨ is from a relatively large alternator, as indicated by the high initial current of 60 A, and for a battery or bank of batteries of large storage capacity or Ampere hour rating, as shown by the relatively slow decline of current which is still an average of 30 A during the second hour of alternator operation. If at the end of the third running hour, more than 50 Ampere hours remain to be recharged, the task to do so may become untolerably slow because the current will continue to decrease and hourly averages will fall further.

Manual alternator controls originally used variable power resistors or rheostats. Fixed power resistors or lamps with switches can also be used. More recently, solid state current regulators have replaced some of the older techniques. Sketch ⑩ shows how a manual alternator control is connected to regulator and field coil in a type P alternator. Although a selector switch can be used to connect the control or the regulator to the field coil, such switch is usually not necessary with the present solid state regulators. In use, extra field current from the control causes an increase

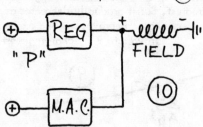

"P"   FIELD   ⑩

in voltage which causes the regulator to switch off. During use of the alternator control, the regulator senses what it is designed to interpret as full batteries. Typically, manual alternator controls decrease the load on the regulator. This is in contrast to some myths here and there.

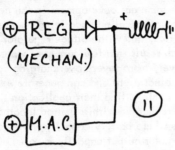

Only if the voltage regulator is a mechanical, relay type, which regulates field current by switching a field contact between plus and ground, one extra precaution is needed. As shown in sketch (11) , a diode must be connected at the regulator field terminal. The diode prevents field current from the manual control from being grounded or shorted out when the mechanical regulator, as designed, connects field terminal to ground when it senses a voltage which normally means that the battery is full. For a regulator with a voltage setting of 14.2 Volt, a voltage of 14.3 V will have it switch. The diode must be able to carry full field current. It does not affect regulator setting since it does not affect regulator plus voltage. All mechanical regulators are external and usually are type P .

Sketch (12) shows how manual controls are connected to type N regulators. Here, increased field current flows through the field coil if current is allowed to bypass the regulator on the way to minus or ground. Many of the type N regulators are internal and almost all of them

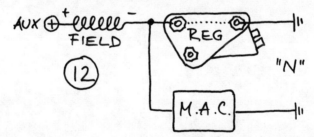

them are solid state types. The sketch is meant to show one of the very popular Delco internal regulators. The dotted line shows the field current path through the regulator to ground. The alternator control here and always is electrically parallel to the voltage regulator.

In operation, an increase in field current usually will increase alternator output voltage slightly above the regulator voltage setting which causes the regulator to switch off. Field current is then solely by manual alternator control. Again, load on the regulator ceases. Only

57

when the manual alternator control is switched off and voltage falls
below the regulator setting will the voltage regulator turn itself on
again, to supply and regulate field current.

    With manual alternator controls comes the risk of overcharging
batteries. Mild overcharging with some gas development in the cells is
carried out on purpose, in the form of so called equalizing charges which
are scheduled for stationary batteries, and with voltage regulator
adjustments in fleet vehicles which result in a few ounces of water lost
from batteries each month. However, more severe overcharging can
result in damaging loss of battery electrolyte and can generate excessive
heat. Usually, manual alternator controls find their application where
relatively large batteries must be recharged within limited lengths of
time. Their application to systems where battery capacity in Ampere
hours is less than three times alternator output capacity is not
advantageous because it does not allow full use of alternator capacity.
Therefore, in practically all instances where a manual alternator control
is useful, the battery capacity will be large enough to prevent serious
battery overcharging.

    Finally, there is an alternator control on the market which
senses battery voltage and, indirectly, the state of charge of the battery
while charging current is flowing. The control allows manual selection
of alternator output current but switches itself off automatically, either
when the battery reaches full charge, or if a charging current is chosen
manually which is too high for the size of the battery.

SPECIFIC VOLTAGE REGULATORS

We have looked at voltage regulators in an earlier section, to see that all of them regulate field current in response to battery voltage. The voltage regulators all have in common to be connected in series with the alternator field coil. All regulate field current, with the ultimate goal of maintaining a specific voltage at the alternator output terminal. Most, if not all regulators work by rapidly switching the field current on and off, achieving greater average field current and alternator output by increasing the "on" time in their on-off switching cycle.

All voltage regulators have at least three terminals : think of them as input, out, and the terminal which measures the voltage which is to be maintained. In this section, we will sketch this basic regulator just as a box with two terminals which are interconnected by a dotted line, and with a third terminal, see the sketch at left. Function of this circuit is to be more or less conductive along the dotted line, depending on the voltage which is being sensed. Many voltage regulators have just these three terminals. However, there are two different ways to put them to use : in the next sketches, the field coil is either at the minus or the plus end of the regulator. Since both are in series, it makes no difference how current is being controlled. See the valve, think of the field coil as a garden hose. The valve can control flow rate , no matter whether it is at the input or output end of the hose.

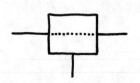

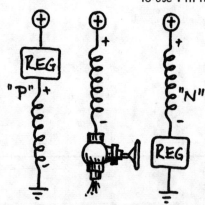

Since we have to distinguish between the two, we have called the left arrangement type "P" : regulator at the Positive side of the field coil, connected plus – regulator – field coil – minus. And we call the arrangement on the right type " N " , regulator at the Negative side of the field coil, connected plus – field coil – regulator – minus.

Caution : several manufacturers make alternators with both type "P" and type "N" voltage regulators . The regulators are not normally interchangeable, and there is no uniform way of identification.

The regulators in sketches 1 and 2 have three terminals each. Both are shown connected to their field coil. Compare with the earlier definition : regulator 1 is on the plus side of the field coil while regulator 2 is on the minus side, between field coil minus terminal and ground. That makes regulator 1 a type "P" and regulator 2 a type "N" . The flow of field current through the regulator is along the dotted

IGN F FIELD COIL
+ "P" REG ①

FIELD COIL ② REG "N"
+

line : we will use this symbol in the regulators in this section to indicate the path for field current which is being controlled. You can view the dotted line as a resistor which the regulator can change as it regulates.

Each of the two regulators needs a third terminal in order to measure voltage, the input variable which the (voltage) regulator is to regulate or keep constant. In regulator ① , the IGN (ignition key) terminal serves two functions : it supplies any needed field current and, at the same time, supplies battery plus voltage which is being measured. To complete this measuring circuit, the third terminal to ground/minus.

In regulator ② , the ground terminal serves two functions : it completes the field current circuit (plus–field coil–regulator–ground), it also serves as minus terminal for the voltage measurement. Since this regulator "sees" battery plus voltage only through the field coil, it needs the third terminal to measure battery plus voltage directly : note the differences .

You wonder why not all alternators use simple (and inexpensive) regulators like these ? There are some necessary functions which here must be taken on by switches, relays, resistors, or diodes but which can be incorporated in the voltage regulator and which will then make it more complex. These functions mainly are the initial exciting of the alternator, operation of a charge pilot light, and automatic switching of regulator and field current, to avoid draining batteries while engines are off.

POWER FOR THE REGULATOR

In the simplest case, a switch is used to connect the voltage regulator
to a battery, to start field current which then allows the alternator to
generate output power. Such switch often is the ignition key switch or
another hand operated switch. It can also be a pressure switch which
automatically connects battery power to the regulator when fuel or oil
pressure of the engine rises as the engine begins to run.

To make alternators self contained units with internal or attached
voltage regulators, and with a minimum of external wiring connections,
there are mainly two methods to automatically send power to regulator
and field. Sketch ③ shows the isolating diode method. The sketch
starts with the three stator terminals which carry alternating current and

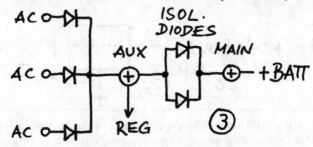

are labeled AC. Then there are the three positive rectifying diodes
with a plus terminal named AUX, for auxiliary terminal, with a
connection to the regulator. Between AUX and MAIN battery output
terminal are isolating diodes which prevent battery current from reaching
the AUX terminal. With the alternator running, AC alternating current
is being rectified and AUX is at plus voltage and supplies the regulator.
Battery charging current and alternator output must pass the isolating
diode(s). When the alternator is off, no switching is necessary since
battery power cannot reach the AUX terminal backwards through the
isolating diodes.

Since the isolating diode or diodes must be able to carry full
alternator output current, they are mounted on a heat sink at the back
of the alternator (Motorola : see sketches), with one diode to about 40 A,
and two diodes to about 55 A. For larger output, isolating diodes become
impractical.

Due to the voltage drop which occurs at diodes, the voltage at
the AUX terminal will be about 0.6 to 1.0 Volt higher than at the main
BAT output terminal while the alternator is in operation. Regulators
which measure the AUX terminal voltage as their input signal cannot be
connected to +BATT without readjustment : they would cause the alternator output voltage to be about one volt higher than designed.

A "diode trio" is another method to feed power to field and regulator automatically. As shown in sketch ④ , an additional group of three diodes is connected directly to the AC stator terminals. The sketch again shows the main plus rectifying diodes with the main output terminals. Then there is the trio of smaller diodes with their own plus terminal which is connected to the regulator or field coil (depending on type, "N" or "P"). The diodes in the diode trio have to be able only to carry the needed field current, they are usually much smaller than the main rectifying diodes or isolating diodes. The diode trio method therefore is used in alternators of all sizes, from those of under 30 A to those well over 100 A. Diode trios are used in the majority of alternators with internal voltage regulators. Often, these smaller diodes are soldered in

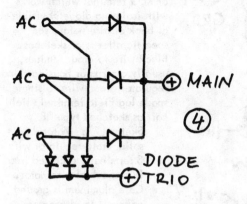

among the main diodes and may be almost invisible until an alternator is fully disassembled. In other cases, the diode trio is a package easily recognized. At left, sketch ⑤ shows life sized a typical Delco diode trio. The schematic at the bottom shows the individual diodes in the package : they are easy to test with a volt ohm meter.

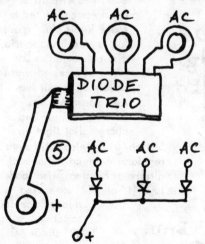

An important difference between the diode trio plus terminal and the isolating diode AUX terminal is that the diode trio plus terminal, with alternator in operation, is more nearly at main output terminal voltage : both terminals are separated by one diode from the AC source, and the voltage drop across diodes is the same for larger or smaller diodes.

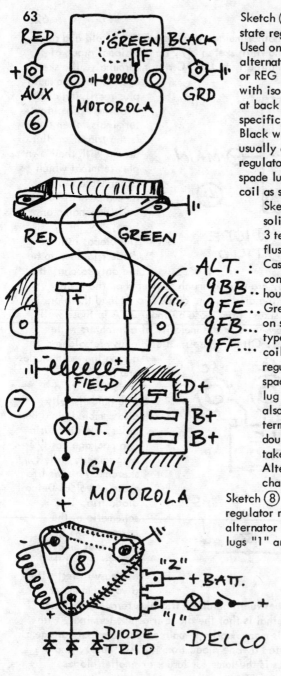

RED

GREEN BLACK

+ AUX

MOTOROLA

GRD

⑥

RED   GREEN

ALT. :
9BB··
9FE··
9FB···
9FF····

+

FIELD

⑦

Ⓧ LT.

IGN

MOTOROLA

D+

B+
B+

⑧

"2" + BATT.

"1" Ⓧ +

DIODE TRIO   DELCO

Sketch ⑥ : Motorola solid state regulator with 3 terminals. Used on many 55 A and smaller alternators. Red wire is on AUX or REG terminal which works with isolating diode(s) visible at back of alternator, see specific alternator sketches. Black wire to ground/minus, usually alternator housing. Under regulator green wire to single spade lug Field terminal, field coil as sketched type "P".

Sketch ⑦ : Motorola solid state regulator with 3 terminals, recessed into flush back of alternator. Case aluminum is ground, connects to alternator housing which is minus. Green wire under regulator on spade lug is Field, type P : see sketch of field coil. Red wire under regulator connected to spade lug is plus, spade lug is plus of diode trio, also connected to D+ terminal recessed next to double B+ output lugs which take common plug. Alternator is excited by charge pilot light on D+ .

Sketch ⑧ : Delco solid state regulator mounted inside back alternator housing, with spade lugs "1" and "2" extending through opening sometimes with "R" stator AC lug terminal. Three molded-in terminals each have hex head screw. Wiring is type N as shown.

Alternators with diode trio or with isolating diode use part of their own output power to supply field current. When they are first started up, there is no output power because there is no field current. And in turn, there would be no field current unless there were some output power first. In some alternators, enough residual magnetism is retained in the steel shaft and iron rotor to make them "self exciting". At sufficient speed, the slightly magnetic rotor generates some AC which is rectified, makes some field current and cycles the alternator into full operation.

All other alternators with diode trio or isolating diodes need a small amount of excite current to start the generating process. This excite current is usually is provided through a charge pilot light or so called idiot light, through a resistor, or a combination of both, sometimes with the use of a relay. The excite current always comes from the battery.

RANGE OF EXCITE CURRENT

An ignition switch or oil pressure switch is normally used to switch the excite current on . The current has to be great enough to have the alternator start generating. It should be as small as possible because the alternator output power can not be reduced below that amount of output which is due to the excite current.

SPECIFIC REGULATORS WITH EXCITE TERMINALS

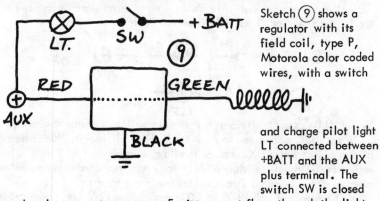

Sketch ⑨ shows a regulator with its field coil, type P, Motorola color coded wires, with a switch

and charge pilot light LT connected between +BATT and the AUX plus terminal. The switch SW is closed when the alternator starts to run. Excite current flows through the light and turns the light on bright. The same current flows through regulator and field coil and causes the initial alternator output. This in turn causes the AUX terminal to rise to full positive voltage which makes the light go off : it now has about full battery voltage at both sides.

Sketch ⑩ shows field coil and voltage regulator in a type N circuit.
A charge indicator light LT with switch SW brings some current from
+BATT through switch and lamp to the auxiliary plus terminal which is
shown here with a diode trio. The initial lamp current excites the

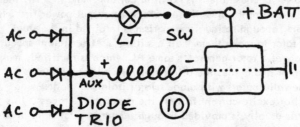

alternator .   Rectified AC through the diode trio then brings the
auxiliary terminal to full plus voltage which extinguishes the light : it
has then approximately full battery voltage at both terminals, current
through the light falls and the light becomes dark.

In both sketches ⑨ and ⑩ the auxiliary terminal could be
operating with either a diode trio or with isolating diode or diodes. The
circuit in sketch 9 is more typical for Motorola alternators with
internal (attached) regulators while sketch ⑩ is typical for many Delco
alternators.

Such external excite current circuits can be used with, or added
to all of the simple 3-terminal voltage regulators. A resistor can be
used in place of the light, or a combination of light and resistor are in
use. 12 V lamps are used in 12 Volt systems. Lamp wattage determins
the lowest speed at which the alternator "cuts in".

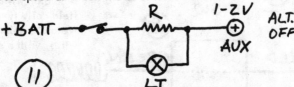

Sketch ⑪ shows ignition or oil pressure switch, resistor R with light
LT in parallel, connected to AUX terminal of alternator. With alternator
off but switch on, AUX terminal should rise to about 1 to 2 Volt. Since
regulator-field coil resistance (AUX to ground resistance) varies between
alternators, only approximate values are given here :
12 Volt system : R about 75 to 300 Ohm, LT a 12 V lamp, about 5 W.
24 Volt system : R about 150 to 600 Ohm, LT a 24 V lamp, about 5 W.

If only a light is used, increase wattage to excite at lower RPM. Also
increase wattage or connect resistor if light does not fully extinguish
when alternator is running and charging or working normally.

Sketch ⑫ shows a Motorola regulator with internal excite resistor. Operation is identical to separate resistors as in sketch ⑪ . Yellow wire is normally connected to ignition or engine key switch or oil pressure

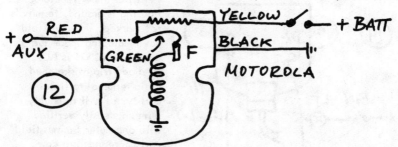

switch. Red wire to AUX terminal at back of alternator, black wire to minus, usually stud terminal on housing. Green wire to field spade lug under regulator. Type P as sketched. Very popular on 30 to 55 A alternators with isolation diodes, see alternator sketches.

   A similar regulator, sketch ⑬ , is made as an external regulator, mounted separately from the alternator and connected

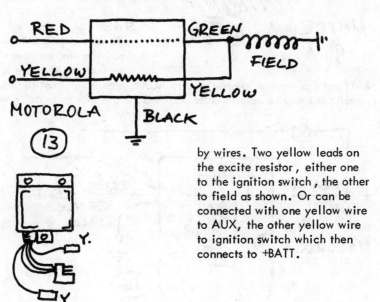

by wires. Two yellow leads on the excite resistor, either one to the ignition switch, the other to field as shown. Or can be connected with one yellow wire to AUX, the other yellow wire to ignition switch which then connects to +BATT.

Sketch ⑭ : attached solid state regulator, recessed flush back Motorola alternators with model numbers beginning with "9" (made in France).

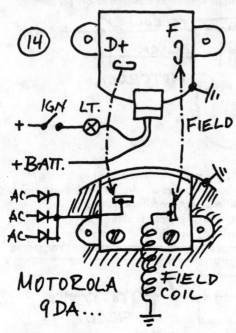

No wires under regulator. Housing is ground, terminals not marked. D+ and Field have matching spade lug connections. D+ is AUX + on diode trio as sketched. Field terminal to field coil type P . If in doubt, terminals easily verified with ohmmeter : minus field coil is grounded to case, field coil resistance is about 4 Ohm.

Plug on regulator has wire to +BATT to sense, and wire to charge indicator light and ignition switch as sketched.

Sketch ⑮ : attached solid state regulator in similar housing as three-wire version. Red wire to +BATT voltage sensing, orange wire to AUX+, charge light not necessary to excite but may be connected as sketched. White wire to switch gives

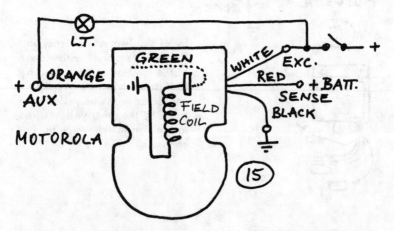

excite current with resistor in regulator. Green wire under regulator connects to Field spade lug, field coil type P .

Sketch ⑯ : Delco external regulator for alternators with "F" "R" parallel lug terminals. Regulator with F-2-3-4 terminals may be electromechanical, with two relay coils, may be hybrid with mechanical relay and solid state regulator circuit, or all solid state.

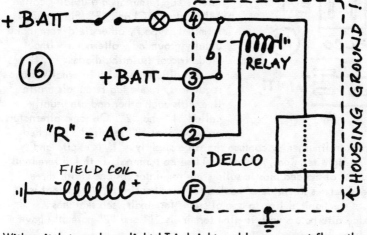

With switch turned on, light LT is bright and lamp current flows through regulator and field coil to excite alternator. Alternator terminal "R" brings AC from stator windings to relay coil. Once alternator is in full operation, relay contacts close and connect +BATT directly to regulator. Lamp then has +BATT at each of its terminals and becomes dark.

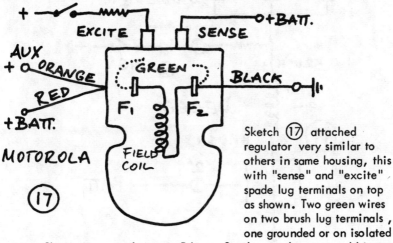

Sketch ⑰ attached regulator very similar to others in same housing, this with "sense" and "excite" spade lug terminals on top as shown. Two green wires on two brush lug terminals, one grounded or on isolated minus. Shown connected as type P here. Similar regulators type N in use on alternators 70 A and larger.

Sketch ⑱ : spade lug connections on Delco alternators (Delco Remy)
are arranged parallel to each other
on alternators for external voltage regulators. Lug terminals are usually called
"R" (stator, AC) and "F" (Field plus
terminal, type P, other field terminal
usually grounded), alternator without
diode trio or isolating diodes.

On alternators with internal voltage
regulators, spade lug terminals are in
line with each other and are usually
called "1" and "2". On some alternators,
an additional "R" terminal, sketched
with broken lines, may confuse the issue slightly. "1" is excite and
charging light terminal, "2" is +BATT sense terminal, both lug terminals
extend out of molded plastic solid state regulator fastened with three
hex head screws to inside of back alternator housing. "R" terminal is
separate mechanical link to one of stator terminals, see sketches.

Delco alternators with in-line terminals "1" and "2" normally have
diode trio. Type N.

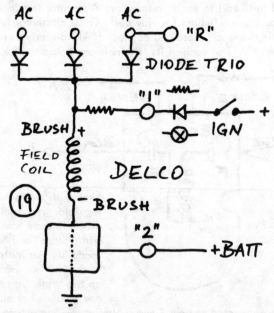

Sketch ⑲ : terminals and internal solid state regulator in Delco
alternators. "R" terminal for tachometers on diesel engines.

Sketch ⑳ : Delco alternators with internal regulator, without spade lug terminals. Main identifying feature is a square black plastic plug as sketched at left, about full size. Plug can be lifted, turned, and pressed

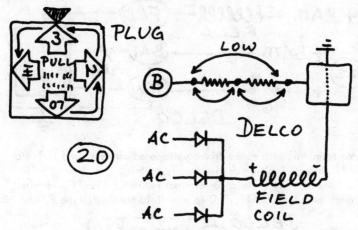

back in place. Plug bypasses or connects two resistors in regulator plus input circuit as shown by arrows in diagram, changes voltage which the voltage regulator maintains at alternator output terminal from LOW to intermediate settings to HIgh. Alternator is self exciting (by residual magnetism in shaft and rotor), has diode trio and molded plastic regulator but no external terminals other than plus and minus output. Type N.

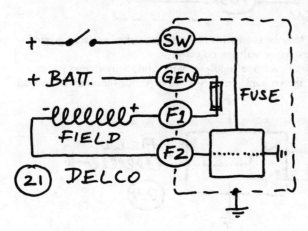

Sketch ㉑ Delco external regulator with SW, GEN, F1 and F2 terminals : housing bracket is ground. Internal fuse can be tested with ohmmeter. Used with older, and recent larger alternators. Type N .

Sketch ㉒ shows a Delco 4-terminal regulator : mounting bracket is ground. Terminals FLD (field type N as shown), BAT (+BATT voltage

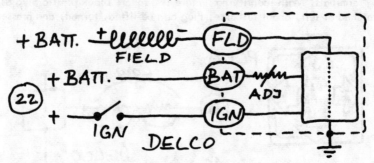

sense terminal) with screw driver voltage adjustment, and IGN (to +BATT through ignition or oil pressure switch).

Sketch ㉓ : Delco 3-terminal regulator with POS terminal through switch to +BATT, FLD to plus field terminal, type P, and NEG

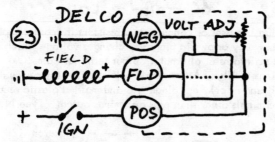

minus terminal. May be used with isolated ground or positive ground alternators. Screwdriver voltage adjustment.

Sketch ㉔ : voltage regulator with plus, minus, and field terminal (type P shown here), and two AC or stator terminals. Diodes in

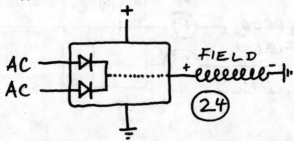

regulator work like diode trio, rectify AC and supply field current. Also made with only one AC terminal and one rectifying diode. Use ohmmeter to identify. Alternator will not have diode trio or AUX terml.

Sketch (25) : possible 5-terminal or 6-terminal regulator with type N field (none of the field brushes grounded or minus), alternator does not have diode trio or AUX terminal with isolating diodes, ignition switch has connection to charge pilot light and/or excite resistor also connected

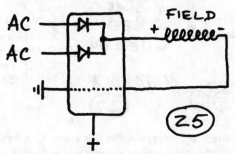

to plus field terminal. Two AC or stator terminals shown with two recti-fying diodes, but may only have one AC terminal and one diode. Use ohmmeter to identify.

Sketch (26) : numbered terminals on external Motorola regulator, color code of wires shown in sketch(27). Switch handles charge light and excite resistor current. Relay powered by stator AC switches +BATT for full field

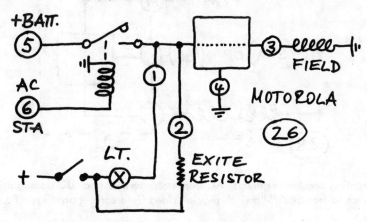

current and to sense battery voltage. Type P.

73

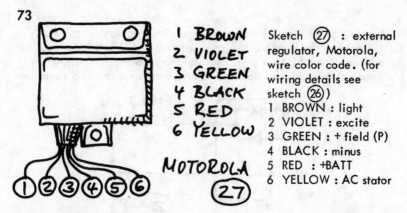

1 BROWN
2 VIOLET
3 GREEN
4 BLACK
5 RED
6 YELLOW

MOTOROLA ㉗

Sketch ㉗ : external regulator, Motorola, wire color code. (for wiring details see sketch ㉖)
1 BROWN : light
2 VIOLET : excite
3 GREEN : + field (P)
4 BLACK : minus
5 RED : +BATT
6 YELLOW : AC stator

Sketch ㉘ : external regulator, Ford, solid state. Can be used with charge Indicator light (shown here) or Ampere meter (sketch ㉙).

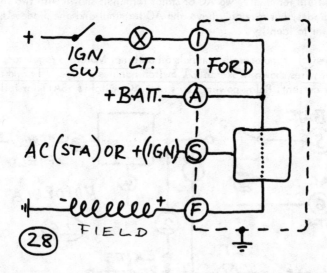

Mounting bracket is ground. AC from stator terminal, or DC from ignition switch to terminal "S" switch regulator and field current on. Type P.

Sketch ㉙ : same solid state regulator as in sketch ㉘ , Ford, here shown connected with Ampere meter which should be a 60-0-60 A meter. Current to accessory electrical equipment is taken off at "X".

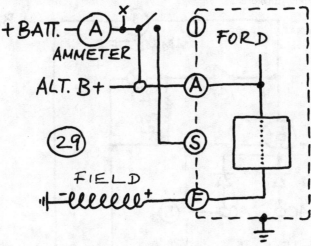

Meter will then show net charging current (alternator output current minus current used by accessory equipment) while alternator is running, or total discharge current when alternator is off.

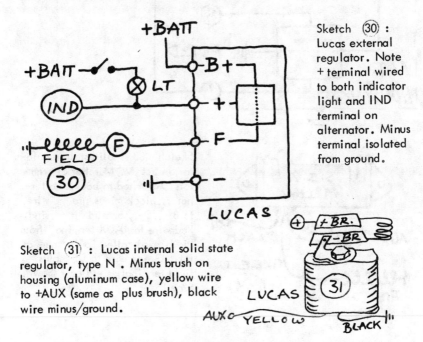

Sketch ㉚ : Lucas external regulator. Note + terminal wired to both indicator light and IND terminal on alternator. Minus terminal isolated from ground.

Sketch ㉛ : Lucas internal solid state regulator, type N . Minus brush on housing (aluminum case), yellow wire to +AUX (same as plus brush), black wire minus/ground.

Sketch ③② : Ford internal regulator, shown with alternator and external wiring details. So called "integral charging system". Can operate with or without ammeter.

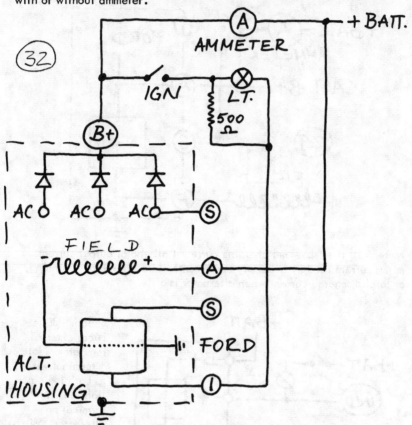

Sketch ③③ : solid state regulator on S.E.V. Marchal alternators. Attached to back of alternator, black minus/ground wire to B− , D− , or stud on housing. Red wire to +AUX terminal (from diode trio) called "61", same as D+ . Green wire to DF, plus field terminal, field coil shown, type P .

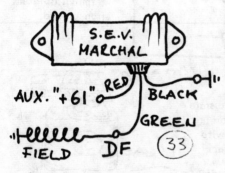

Sketch ③④ : external, mechanical regulator, Nippondenso, with five color coded wires shown as wide bars in the sketch. Consists of two almost identical coils with single pole double throw contacts each. Ignition switch brings +BATT voltage to charge light LT and left relay coil which pulls contact arm, to bring lamp current through resistor R to field wire . After alternator has been excited and is running, field

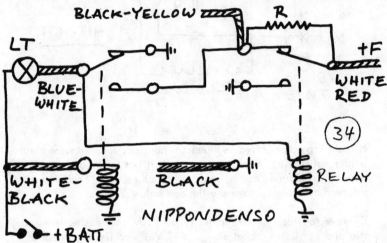

current comes from +AUX via Black-Yellow wire. Coil and contacts at right are voltage regulator, coil begins to pull only after voltage rises above initial +BATT voltage.

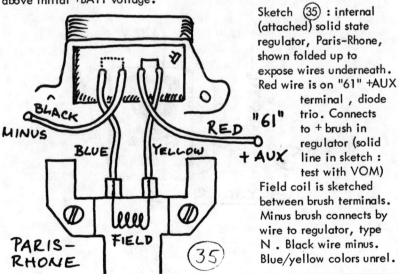

Sketch ③⑤ : internal (attached) solid state regulator, Paris-Rhone, shown folded up to expose wires underneath. Red wire is on "61" +AUX terminal , diode trio. Connects to + brush in regulator (solid line in sketch : test with VOM) Field coil is sketched between brush terminals. Minus brush connects by wire to regulator, type N . Black wire minus. Blue/yellow colors unrel.

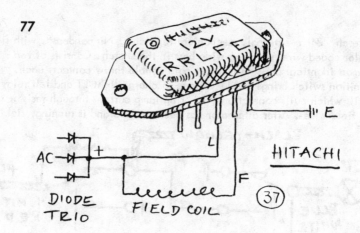

AC

DIODE
TRIO

FIELD COIL

HITACHI

③⑦

Hitachi regulator potted in aluminum housing, located near brush holder, difficult to access, type N . If it has failed and does not short F to ground, can be replaced by other type N regulators mounted outside, for example the one below .

Chrysler regulator, 3 terminals, type N . Metal housing is ground, two pins in plastic socket are plus 12 Volt and field terminal as sketched. Steel housing without mounting feet measures about 2.5 by 3.5 inches, about half inch thick without connector socket, circuit is cast in resin.

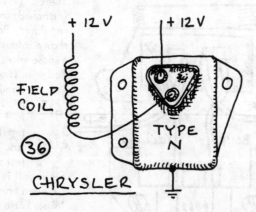

FIELD
COIL

+ 12 V   + 12 V

TYPE
N

③⑥

CHRYSLER

REPAIRS

Let us divide repairs to the alternator and regulator into two groups and call them "standard" and "non-standard" repairs. Standard repairs will usually consist of testing to identify a faulty component, and of the replacement with a new component . Standard repairs are guided by service bulletins and lists of part numbers which the manufacturers of the alternator publish for that purpose. Such bulletins usually give test procedures and specifications for the results. They also usually tell in great detail how to disassemble and reinstall. With the model number of the alternator or regulator, the part number of the faulty component is then used to purchase a new one. The new part may come from the manufacturer of the alternator or from companies which specialize in making replacement parts. Such repairs are bound to be straight forward, the result predictable, they are the recommended route whenever possible.

Into the group of standard repairs also belong the so called rebuilt alternators. These are the more popular makes and models of alternators , both imported and domestic brands. Cores, which are used alternators, are disassembled and a standard list of replacement parts is installed, usually including bearings, diodes, brushes, internal voltage regulators. Rebuilt alternators are reported to perform as the originals and are often a very economical alternative to repairs.

Non-standard repairs are the ones we want to look at here : repairs which become necessary to an alternator of unknown brand and model, without the help of an applicable service bulletin, testing procedures, parts lists, or special tools. Repairs which may help when there is no other help around.

TROUBLE SHOOTING

This is the essential first step. Trouble shooting points out a faulty component in the alternator or regulator, or it tells you that the trouble is not there but rather in other associated equipment or wiring. You can avoid trouble shooting only if you replace the whole alternator, and then only if the trouble was in fact in the alternator.

TESTING WITH THE ALTERNATOR ON THE ENGINE

We have talked about it before : the alternator MUST be connected to a battery or other load whenever it is running. With any field current but with the output disconnected, high voltage can be generated which can distroy voltage regulator and diodes.

ALTERNATOR OUTPUT TESTS

ENGINE OFF : If there is an ammeter, check its wiring. Both meter terminals, as well as alternator output terminal and battery plus terminal measure same voltage against minus or engine ground. Only exception : charging diodes or isolating diodes will block.

Check if there is any new wiring which allows current to bypass the ammeter without being measured.

Without ammeter, do not try to patch one in, do not disconnect output wire from battery or alternator : too risky, may interrupt output and cause damage.

ENGINE RUNNING : compare details in section on voltage regulator testing. Signs for alternator output are increased brightness of lights when engine speed is increased from slow idle, increasing battery voltage by one or more volts, engine off to engine running, same increase at alternator output terminal. With charging or isolating diodes : alternator output terminal shows no voltage versus ground with engine off, comes to battery voltage or higher with engine and alternator running. Another sign for alternator output is gassing, bubbles, in cells of the battery.

There are inductive ammeters which are clamped on a wire and which respond to the magnetic field from direct current. Similarly, a

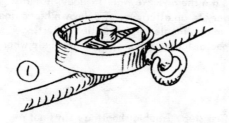

compass will show if there is current flowing : as in the sketch, hold compass near wire, let needle settle while no current flows, then note change with current. To get a rough idea of magnitude of current, test the compass with a wire to a light or other equipment which you can switch on and off. Use any of these output tests to signal you in the next field current test.

FIELD CURRENT TEST

ALTERNATOR HAS EXTERNAL VOLTAGE REGULATOR : There will be a field terminal at the outside of the alternator. Search through the alternator sketches, look for a terminal "F" . Disconnect regulator wires from the alternator, do not short any of them. Make a test light from a lamp of 10 Watt or more (smaller lights allow too little current).

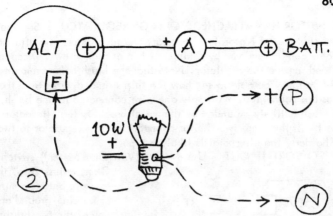

Connect the test light as sketched at "P" , between the field terminal
of the alternator and plus, for example at the plus output terminal.
With the engine running, type P alternators should generate some
output current due to the field current which is supplied through the
lamp. The lamp may or may not actually become bright. If the lamp
wattage is too low, not enough field current may flow to give you a
positive indication of alternator output current.

      Connect the test light between field terminal and ground or
minus, as shown at "N" in sketch ②. Alternators of type N when
running, should respond with output current. The lamp may glow or
become bright : unimportant . The only response we want to see is
alternator output current.

      Most alternators with external voltage regulators in the past have
been type P . There are exceptions, for example Chrysler alternators,
see the regulator number ③⑦ in the regulator section. Most other type
N alternators have internal voltage regulators.

RESULTS : If the alternator had no output with its own voltage
regulator but does generate output current with the test light, the
alternator's main function is all right. If the alternator supplies the
regulator by auxiliary plus terminal and diode trio, you may reconnect
the voltage regulator but connect its plus terminal to battery plus,
instead of the alternator auxiliary terminal, or bring plus voltage to
the auxiliary terminal with a test wire. If that brings back normal
performance, test alternator diode trio, also read section on excitation,
check pilot light, try additional excite current.

ALTERNATOR HAS ATTACHED VOLTAGE REGULATOR : See the various sketches of Motorola alternators and regulators. The attached regulator can be removed by taking out two or four screws. Disconnect wires and remove the regulator. Note that the brush holder remains in place : you may be able to see how the thin stranded wires from the brushes are connected. With only one wire connected to one brush, the other brush is likely grounded by the metal bracket, the alternator is a type P . If there are two similar connections from regulator to two brush holders, the alternator is likely a type N .

HOW TO SORT IT OUT : Use a VOM (Volt Ohm Meter), switch to

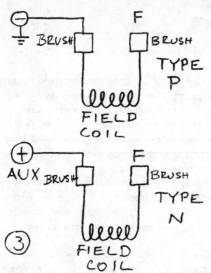

Ohm, adjust zero, then measure between minus or housing/ground and any of the two brushes or field terminal(s). If the reading is near zero Ohm, alternator is a type P , see the sketch : one brush is grounded, field coil resistance is only about 4 Ohm so both brushes are near ground.

If there are two brush terminals, measurement to minus/ground shows high Ohm for both, the alternator is a type N, see the sketch. The connection from a plus auxiliary terminal to one of the brushes may be through the regulator wires which you removed : test with the Ohm meter . One brush wire connected to plus regulator wire : near zero reading on the meter.

Make a test light from a lamp of 10 Watt or more, connect between field terminal F (you may search : only the correct terminal will give alternator output, no harm if you touch wrong terminal) and plus for a type P alternator, or between field terminal F and minus/ground for a type N alternator. Note sketch ② . The current through the lamp should generate alternator output current with engine running. If you see the signs for output current, trouble is in the regulator or its wiring, or in the alternator auxiliary terminal and diode trio. See details for separate test of the regulator in the voltage regulator section.

ALTERNATOR HAS COMBINED REGULATOR-BRUSH HOLDER : Even though the assembly is easy to remove, as on Bosch alternators, no separate test of alternator on engine is practical. However, note auxiliary plus terminal D+ or "61" : connect test light with 10 Watt lamp between battery plus and D+ or 61 and run engine. If that gives some alternator output current, auxiliary diodes may have failed.

The section on voltage regulators gives tests for the regulator.

ALTERNATOR HAS INTERNAL REGULATOR : a large number of these alternators are the type N . Many have a so called TEST HOLE which is normally at the back housing of the alternator, near brush holder and regulator . The hole is located directly over a sheet metal conducter or tab which is in contact with the minus brush, see the details of type N alternators. With the alternator running, a small metal tool can be used to ground the minus brush to alternator housing

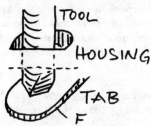 for a brief moment. This bypasses the voltage regulator and allows maximum field current to flow which results in maximum alternator output current if the main alternator components are in order. The alternator sketches show the test hole on Delcotron and some other alternator brands. CAUTION : extra stress is generated, alternator may overheat in a minute or less, and you may be poking into the wrong hole. Even if the alternator responds with output, it will still have to be taken off to test the internal regulator. You could do all testing then.

VOLTAGE REGULATOR SETTING TEST

If the alternator itself is working, you can test the voltage regulator setting by running the alternator long enough to reach full charge of a small (reaches full charge sooner) battery, then measuring the voltage at the alternator output terminal while the alternator is still running at relatively fast speed. Low settings make it difficult to recharge low batteries. High settings cause decomposition of water in battery cells and make more frequent refilling with distilled water necessary. See details in earlier sections of the book.

If the alternator is not working and the voltage regulator must be tested by itself, use the test in the voltage regulator section : connect to a lamp in place of field coil, and to a battery plus charger as a source of direct current of sufficiently high voltage to make the regulator switch. Typical setting for 12 V systems is 14.0 to 14.4 Volt.

SUMMARY : TESTING WITH ALTERNATOR ON ENGINE

We have tested for alternator output as such, and with field current supplied through a test light instead of the voltage regulator. The output power generating components of all alternators are similar and consist of stator and main rectifying diodes together with rotor and field coil. If there was output current in the tests up to this point, no matter what brand or design : we know that the stator coils are not shorted, none of the diodes are shorted although one or more diodes may have become open (non conducting) and stator wires may have broken. Other tests will tell us that. We found the regulator working or found it faulty : if so, see the following repair recommendations.

TESTING : ALTERNATOR TAKEN OFF ENGINE

This may be your first chance to clearly inspect the alternator. Turn the pulley by hand : you will hear the sound of the brushes riding on the slip rings, unless the alternator is a design without brushes (such as Niehoff, Marchal, large Delco-Remy), you have a chance to hear noise from bad bearings.

ALL ALTERNATORS : To verify what we may already know, test the main recifying diodes with a VOM. Sketch ① shows the three AC

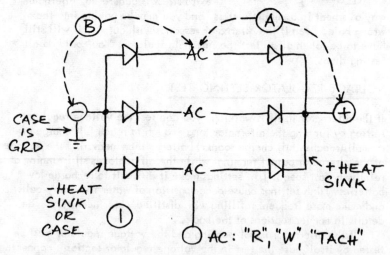

terminals of "Y" or "Delta" stators, the three positive and negative rectifying diodes with their plus and minus terminals. Minus may be grounded to case, and there may be a stator terminal with AC, called "R" or "TACHometer" or "W". If there is'nt, you can make contact to the stator in another way : see sketch ② and look through the vent holes in the back. Look for one of the positive diodes . They are mounted on a heat sink which is the plus output conductor (verify with Ohm meter) , and the tip of the diodes is part of the stator, see sketch 1 and earlier sketches. If the housing is ground, minus, you may see the three negative diodes pressed directly into the housing which serves as their heat sink.

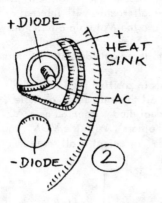

Switch the VOM to the lowest Ohm range, adjust zero, then measure between AC and minus terminal or ground as shown at "B", and between AC and plus output terminal as at "A", sketch ① . We are testing diodes which conduct in one direction and block in the other. Use the Ohm meter first in one direction and read, then exchange the wires and take

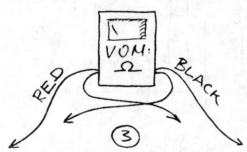

another reading, as shown in sketch ③ . The internal battery of the VOM, usually 1.5 or 3 Volt, will give readings of 200 to 1000 Ohm in one direction, and infinite Ohm in the other, O.K. Never mind whether red or black VOM wire gave the low reading, the diodes will not have switched their polarity. But look out for readings near zero Ohm : they indicate diodes which have failed by becoming shorted. A single shorted diode among the three plus or minus diodes will disable the whole alternator, an open diode will only reduce output. See section on diodes.

AUXILIARY DIODES, DIODE TRIO : The arrangement in sketch ④
is typical for most alternators with internal voltage regulators and plus
auxiliary terminal (called 1 , REG, D+, L, 61) , a large group which
includes Delco-Remy, some Motorola, Bosch, Lucas, Hitachi, Marchal,
Mitsubishi, Nippondenso, Paris-Rhone alternators with internal or
attached regulators. Main exception are the Motorola alternators with
isolating diode, covered in sketch ⑤ . Some large alternators may
have a diode trio assembly attached to three outside stator AC terminals,
for example Leece-Neville.

   The sketch shows the three main positive rectifying diodes for
orientation. The diode trio may have all three diodes in a single
package (Delco, Motorola) or individual diodes mounted near AC
terminals or main diodes (Hitachi and others). With the VOM, you
can detect any shorted auxiliary diode , or detect if all three have

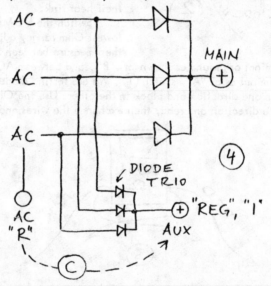

failed by becoming open. Individual diodes will be tested later.
Switch to lowest Ohm range, adjust zero, then measure between any
stator AC terminal (R, W, TACH, or main diode tip, sketch ②)
and the auxiliary plus terminal (1, D+, 61, L), as at "C" , again
measure in both directions, see sketch ③ . One reading should be
a few hundred to about 1000 Ohm, the other reading infinite (meaning
no conductivity) . A very low Ohm reading indicates one or more
shorted diodes.

AUXILIARY TERMINAL WITH ISOLATING DIODE(S) : MOTOROLA
It will help you to look at the appearance of the isolating diode heat
sink which which carries one, two, or three press-fitted diodes, is
made from aluminum sheet or cast, has a unique section-of-a-ring
shape and is mounted on the outside back of some Motorola alternators.

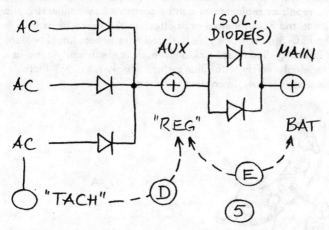

Note that the auxiliary REG terminal is electrically in the place where
other alternators have their main output terminal. In this arrangement,
the isolating diode(s) (two shown in sketch ⑤) allow alternator output
current to reach the main plus terminal and battery. But when the
alternator is off, battery current is prevented from reaching the REG
terminal and be waisted as regulator and field current.

Use the VOM, Ohm range, zero adjusted, as shown in sketch ⑤
at "D" and "E" , measuring in both directions (see sketch ③).
At both places, you should get one reading of infinite Ohm (no
conductivity) and one reading of about 200 to 1000 Ohm. Any
reading of near zero Ohm indicates a shorted diode. Infinite Ohms at
"D" would mean that all three main plus rectifying diodes have failed
by becoming open, very unlikely. Infinite readings at "E" would
mean that the isolating diode(s) is open, or all two or three are open.

With two or three isolating diodes on the heat sink, individual
diodes can be tested after removing the isolating diode heat sink : free
the nuts, note where the insulating shoulder washers belong. Open
soldered diode connections under heat sink, test separated diodes.

If the isolating diode test "E" shows a shorted diode, the
alternator can still work normally except that the REG terminal will be
about 0.6 V lower than with the isolating diode in tact. This will

affect the operation of the voltage regulator which is designed to take the voltage drop at the isolating diode into account. The regulator will now maintain an alternator output voltage about 0.6 V lower than before which may leave batteries less well charged and which will reduce charging current.

If the isolating diode is found to be open, or damaged in some other way, repair or replacement can be postponed by connecting the output wire to the REG terminal or, better, to the post with nut nearest the REG terminal (the side with red wire to regulator) which holds the isolating diode heat sink and which is electrically same as the REG terminal, verify with Ohm meter. See sketch ⑥ . Note that the heat sink is hot, in contact with the REG stud.

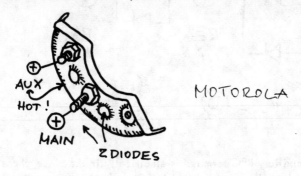

MOTOROLA

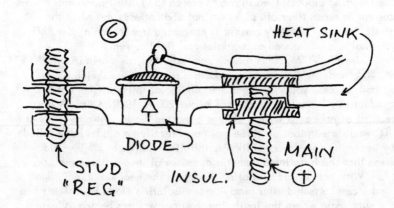

TYPE P WITH DIODE TRIO : Relatively rare. Schematic is shown in
sketch ⑦ . If regulator is attached instead of inside back kousing,
access to brushes or brush terminals may let you test the regulator :
disconnect plus brush or take out brush holder . Connect test light to
plus brush terminal, supply power by connection to auxiliary plus
terminal of alternator, or directly to regulator. Follow test procedure
in voltage regulator section.

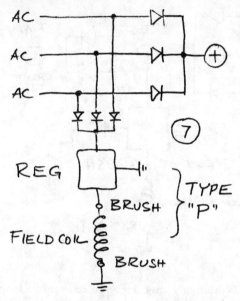

Connect VOM between positive brush terminal and minus/ground,
switch to lowest Ohm range. Turn pulley by hand and watch for large
changes in meter readings which would indicate oily or dirty brushes
and slip rings. Very easy to clean if brush holder is removeable from
outside. Use cloth wetted with naphtha, paint thinner, acetone, all
very flammable. Other alternators : disassemble, see instructions next
section .

TYPE P WITH ISOLATING DIODE : Many Motorola models in sizes up to 55 Ampere, some larger models. Usually have attached voltage regulator, brush holders under the regulator which are removeable and allow outside access to slip rings, characteristic shape of the isolating diode heat sink mounted to outside of back housing, see sketch ⑥ .

Regulator connections are shown in sketch ⑧ . Regulator may have additional terminals, see examples of Motorola regulators in that section.

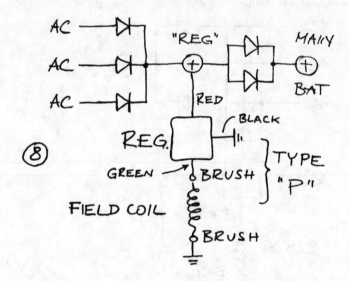

Trouble shooting is relatively easy since you can remove the voltage regulator. Test brushes and field coil by connecting the VOM, Ohm range, to the single spade lug on the brush holder, and to minus/ground. Field coil resistance is about 4 Ohm. Turn the pulley by hand : large changes of meter reading indicate dirty slip rings and brushes or possibly worn brushes. Investigate, clean (cloth wetted with solvent).

With brush holder removed, turn the pulley by hand again, feel, and listen to bearings.

Note soft felt or cork gasket under regulator. Make certain it gets back in place. The gasket seals the space around slip rings and brushes and is essential in environments with possible flammable or explosive atmosphere. In other applications it may keep out abrasive dust.

TYPE N WITH DIODE TRIO : All alternators in this very large group have internal or attached solid state voltage regulators. The group includes many hundred Delcotron models, many by Motorola made here (numbers start with 8) or in France (numbers start with 9), all Bosch alternators with attached regulator-brush holder unit, all Hitachi and Mitsubishi with internal regulator, probably most small to medium sized alternators used in cars and trucks if with internal voltage regulator. The applicable wiring diagram is sketch ⑨ .

   With the alternator in hand, we can do a few tests before disassembling the alternator. Many of the alternators in this group will have a test hole. We can connect the Ohm meter between stator AC terminal "R" and the auxiliary plus terminal ("1" on Delcotrons, D+, 61, L on others) and test the diode trio, as outlined earlier. We can

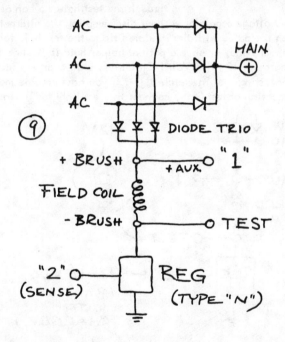

now also test brushes and field coil : insulate most of the metal tip of one of the meter probes with a length of thin plastic tubing, or with tape, see sketch ⑩ . Leave only the lowest end of the tip exposed and use this probe to make contact with the minus brush terminal by inserting the tip into the test hole. This time, we want to keep from making contact with the housing at the same time, hence the plastic tube. Compare the earlier sketch in the Field Current Test section.

With one VOM probe in contact with the tab under the test hole, make contact with the "1" (or D+ etc.) terminal and measure field coil and brush resistance. If you see large changes when you turn the pulley by hand, make sure that is not due to shaky contact inside the test hole. If you detect dirty or worn brushes, most of the alternators in this group will have to be opened for access to brushes. Exception: a few french alternators have no brushes, rare, and of no significant advantage.

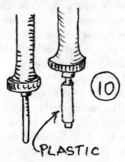

PLASTIC

With the same connection through the test hole we can also test the internal voltage regulator without disassembling the alternator. Try to fasten the probe with the insulated tip to the test hole tab with tape and rubber band, or have a patient helper hold it. Connect test light and source of 12 to 15 Volt DC (battery with charger, section on regulator testing) as in sketch ⑪ . If you have trouble making a good connection at test hole, connect the test light to "1" instead.

DIODE TRIO

+ AUX

FIELD COIL

+12V

"1"

O TEST

⑪ REG — "2" ← 12–15 VDC (BATTERY WITH CHARGER)

"N"

With light between plus 12 V and TEST, or with field coil in tact, to "1" (or L, D+ ... plus aux. terminal), light should be on. Connect source of plus 12 to 15 Volt to the "sense" terminal "2" (Delco) and increase voltage slowly. Somewhere around 14 V the light should go out : regulator O.K., compare details in regulator test section, repeat the test a few times.

DISASSEMBLING THE ALTERNATOR

There are several reasons to open the alternator. Mainly, they are :
ACCESS TO BRUSHES and slip rings : applies to alternators with
internal voltage regulator which do not allow direct access to brushes
from outside. Applies to Delco alternators except larger brushless types,
Hitachi and Mitsubishi alternators with internal regulator, others. Note
that many alternators with attached voltage regulator have removeable
brush holders directly under the regulator, accessible from outside :
Motorola, Bosch, Leece-Neville, Paris-Rhone, others .
ACCESS TO DIODE TRIO or auxiliary diodes, to test individual
diodes in the diode trio or to replace , applies to some Motorola, all
Delco with internal regulators, Bosch, Hitachi, Marchal, Mitsubishi,
and others, all having a plus auxiliary terminal called D+, 61, L, 1 ...
ACCESS TO MAIN DIODES and stator windings, to test individual
diodes and wiring, access to bearings : applies to almost all. Only in
some larger Delco and Motorola alternators can main diodes be removed
at outside.
ACCESS TO INTERNAL REGULATOR : Note that internal voltage
regulators can be tested from outside, with alternator disconnected and
with test wires and test lamp connected to plus aux. terminal, sense
terminal, and ground. See details in earlier section on trouble shooting.
Internal regulators are easy to remove and replace in Delco alternators
but much more difficult in Hitachi and Mitsubishi models. Note that
faulty internal regulators can usually be replaced with other external
voltage regulators. This applies to the attached regulators as well, as
long as a separate brush holder remains in place : more difficult to do
with Bosch where regulator and brush holder are an integral unit.

HOW TO DISASSEMBLE

The alternator in almost all cases consists of a back housing usually of
aluminum, a stator assembly with a laminated iron core which is visible
at the outside, and a front housing of aluminum, or of steel in some
larger alternators. Front housing is the one with the pulley. Front and
back housing are held together with three or four through bolts, and the
stator is clamped between the two housing parts. The through bolts are
usually very long and thin, sometimes run over the outside of the stator,
sometimes out of sight through holes in housings and stator. Heads of
these bolts sometimes are at the face of the front housing but more
often at the rear housing. Since the bolts are evenly spaced, there
usually are several possible positions for back housing on front housing :
mark back, stator, and front housing at side before disassembling.

This applies to alternators with so called "spool mount" only, where mounting bracket is on the front housing only, see sketch ① : you

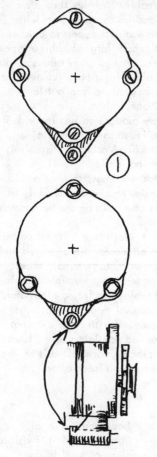

can usually turn the back housing (together with stator) to best suit the space on your engine. With four through bolts, there are four possible positions, three with three, which let you choose the best way for wires and plugs on the alternator.

If you want to change the back housing without taking the alternator apart, caution : the brushes must not come off slip rings. Take out through bolts, then turn only, do not pull apart and push back together which will break off brushes. Back housing and stator must remain together because stator wires are connected to back housing.

TO OPEN, use two screw drivers and pry apart at opposite places at same time. STATOR must stay with BACK HOUSING. Insert screwdrivers between front housing and stator.
CAUTION : do not damage stator wires with tools. Do not change your mind and push back together which will damage brushes.

Lift pulley and front housing, with rotor and slip rings out of back housing-and-stator, see sketch ② .

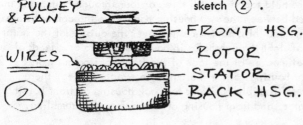

PULLEY & FAN — FRONT HSG.
WIRES → — ROTOR
— STATOR
② — BACK HSG.

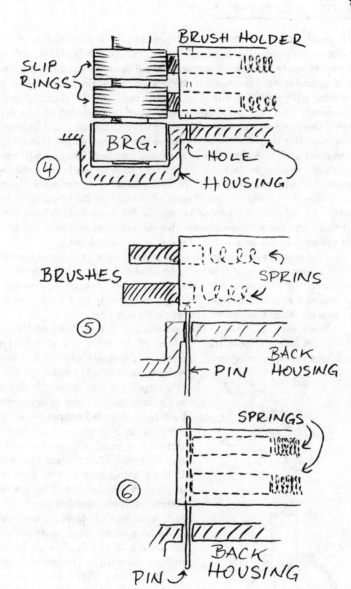

BRUSHES AND PIN HOLE

This applies to alternators with internal regulator and brushes which are not accessible from the outside (Delco, Hitachi, Mitsubishi, others). As you separate the front housing with pulley and rotor from the back housing and stator, brushes will be pushed out of the brush holder as the rotor with shaft and slip rings is removed, see sketches 4 and 5 . Alternators with rear ball bearing will have that bearing remain on the shaft. The bearing has same diameter as the slip rings, and brushes slide over slip rings and bearing as the shaft is pulled out (Hitachi, Mitsubishi). Alternators with rear needle bearings (Delco) will have cage with needles/rollers stay in the rear housing while only the shaft comes out, with grease. AUTION : keep bearing components clean.

Sketch 4 shows a shaft with slip rings and ball bearing. In sketch 5 , the springs behind brushes in the brush holder have pushed out : you can see why we cannot change our mind at this stage and just reassemble the alternator. Brushes would break off.

Alternators in this group have a small hole in the rear housing which allows a pin or stiff wire to be used to hold back the brushes until after the alternator has been reassembled. The pin is then pulled out and releases the brushes. Pulling it out slowly will let you hear the two clicks as each brush settles on its slip ring.

There are variations to this design. Delco type 116 and 136 alternators (outside looks like 10-SI or 15-SI series, see sketches) have their brushes on rotating arms, sketch 7 , instead of the usual brush

holder. Each arm is forced toward the slip rings by a leaf spring. Both arms are plastic, each brush is connected by a thin stranded copper wire. Both arms are on a common metal shaft with slotted flat head, threaded into the rear housing. From the position shown in the sketch, arms must be bent out of the way and held back by pin before alternator is reassembled.

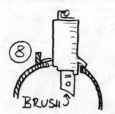

Some brush holders do not have a pin hole on the inner most surface so that the retaining pin must be put in from the outside (Mitsubishi, others) which is more difficult since you must do that while pushing the brushes back into the housing. In this case, start with the outer, lower brush.

The brush in sketch 8 has pin hole but upper holder does not. Note that brush is off center : alternator runs clockwise. Fancy that .

TESTING INDIVIDUAL MAIN DIODES

With the alternator opened up, we can test each diode by itself. There are six main rectifying diodes : three on a common heat sink which is the plus terminal, and another three, built differently, on a common heat sink which is the minus terminal, often the alternator housing itself. Plus diodes are built to have their cathode at their mounting surface or base. Minus diodes have the anode as base, see section on diodes.

There will be three AC stator terminals. In Delco alternators, they are usually located close together, in a row, on the rectifyer bridge which has plus and minus finned heat sinks immediately adjacent, see sketch with Delco alternators. Each AC or stator terminal will look

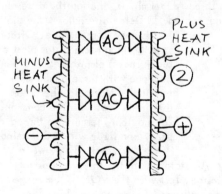

like sketch (1) : two stator wires (if it is a "Delta" stator, see details), then one terminal of the diode trio shown here as the small diode, then underneath in the bridge assembly one plus and one minus diode, shown here with the plus and minus terminals.

To test each diode, take the three nuts off all three AC terminals, bend stator wire terminals up, then bend diode trio terminals up, out of contact with the AC studs. What we have then is shown in

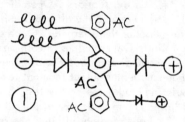

sketch (2) : each of the three AC stud terminals have one diode each to the plus and minus heat sink. Use the VOM, in lowest Ohm range, zero adjusted, and take Ohm measurements . Red wire to plus heat sink or plus main terminal, then black wire to each AC stud. Then exchange red and black meter wires and do all three measurements again.

Then do all that between minus heat sink or terminal and the AC stud terminals. For each diode, one Ohm value should be infinite, one should be a few hundred Ohm, the usual diode test with the VOM .

Other alternators often have plus and minus heat sinks as semi circles around the outer edge of the back housing, tucked under the stator windings as you look into the opened alternator. There will be wires or metal strip conductors which connect stator to the tips of diodes. The connections then are usually soldred.

Identifying the AC terminals of the six main diodes is easy with the Ohm meter : all six terminals will have near zero Ohm from any one to any other (in reality, the very low resistance of the stator windings, lowest with high alternator Amp rating). To measure Ohms of individual diodes, solder connections in this design have to be unsoldered, the readings taken in both directions, then wires soldered back on with some additional rosin core solder. Note that shorted diodes (faulty because conducting in both directions) disable the alternator and can be detected from the outside, see earlier sections . Open diodes (which are not conducting in any direction) reduce the alternator output current but may not completely disable the alternator. Open diodes are detected in this test, by infinite Ohm readings in both directions. Measurement is between minus terminal and three tips of minus diodes, in both directions, and between main plus output terminal (exception : Motorola alternators with isolating diode, see earlier test, here use REG plus auxiliary terminal instead) and three tipe of plus diodes, in both directions. Diode is O.K. if one reading infinite, one reading a few hundred Ohm.

TESTING INDIVIDUAL DIODES IN DIODE TRIO

After disconnecting from the three AC terminals, the fourth, different output terminal may remain connected. In Delco alternators, the diode trio is easy to recognize. Often, it is the long rectangular plastic block shown elsewhere, or other package with three plus one terminals. Motorola alternators use diode trios with the common (plus output) terminal a threaded stud, and three wire AC terminals.

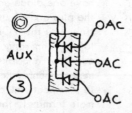

Sketch ③ shows a diode trio, disconnected from AC stator, with the three individual diodes as they are arranged inside. Test with the VOM, Ohm range, zero adjusted, between common plus and each freed AC lug. Then same points again but with meter leads reversed, see earlier explanation. Each diode should have one infinite reading and one reading of a few hundred Ohm. Look for open diodes (infinite in both directions) since any shorted diode would have been detected earlier.

TESTING THE STATOR WINDINGS

There are three possible kinds of trouble, all are apparently rare :
1. Short between windings and stator core or ground,
2. Short between wires, from one wire to another, and
3. Open windings, such as a broken wire .

The first is most easily detected, even from the outside. Stator and all
diodes remain connected. Use the lowest Ohm range of the VOM,
test between any AC stator terminal and the metal body of the
laminated iron stator . You may use the tachometer terminal, or other

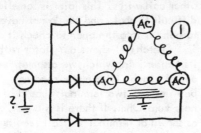

outside AC terminal by
other names (R, W, STA)
or reach the tip of one
of the plus diodes.

In alternators with
minus on cas/ground, we
are measuring across the
minus diodes, sketch ①.
Here, the Ohm readings
should be infinite in one
direction, a few hundred Ohm in the other (as we measure the forward
direction of the minus diodes) but never near zero which would indicate
a winding short to ground.

In the more rare alternators with isolated ground, both Ohm
readings should be infinite, indicating no conductivity.

Interference in this test comes from a shorted minus diode which
would give us the same indication as a winding short in the minus–on–
ground alternator : obvious, look at sketch ① . A hot alternator with
low output would be the result of either short.

A short between wires of the stator windings is much more
difficult to detect . A low range Ohm meter would be necessary, and
even then a short within one coil would be hard to find and its effect
on alternator performance hard to measure. But shorts between any of
the three coils could drastically reduce performance. Shorts such as
these appear to be rare.

Open windings or broken wires also are difficult to find
with the VOM but are more easily found by inspection. Since the solid
copper wires of the stator are vulnerable to break where they can move
or vibrate, look for likely such places.

Your inspection will show you if the stator is a "Y" or "DELTA"
type : the Delta stator in sketch ① has two wires from two coils come
together at some point at the rectifying diodes. You should be able to
see three terminals with two solid copper lacquer insulated wires. These
joints would have to be opened to measure conductance in each coil.

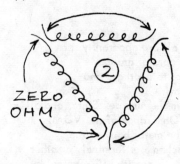

ZERO
OHM

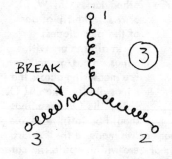

BREAK

With the Delta windings disconnected at the terminals, Ohm readings of near zero Ohm should show at the three places in sketch ② , for three healthy coils.

You can recognize a "Y" stator by the three AC terminals each with a single solid copper wire, and by a joint, the center of the Y , usually crimped, and tucked in among the other coil wires. This joint is sometimes difficult to spot, and we do not have to bend it into the open to chech it .

Sketch ③ shows a Y stator with its center joint which, we assume, is out of reach. Ohm meter readings between any two terminals should be near zero Ohm. If there is a break, as shown at terminal 3 , all readings from 3 to the other two terminals would be high (infinite).

Unfortunately, locating such break only helps by identifying a problem. Finding and reconnecting such broken wire is almost impossible since the coil wire is stiff, tightly wound, with loops of different coils overlapping, and with the wire hard to solder due to its lacquer insulation.

The effect of a break in the stator windings is a reduction of alternator output. The alternator would tend to become hotter only because the voltage regulator will tend to achieve normal output which places a greater load on the working coils and their diodes.

RIPPLE TEST

If you have an opportunity to run an alternator under conditions which you can repeat, you may be able to measure a difference between normal operation and operation with a stator wire break or with a faulty, open rectifying diode. Use the VOM, switched to a low AC range, such as 10 VAC . Note alternator or engine speed, output current , and the size of the battery. Take a measurement between alternator output terminal and ground. The indication of an AC voltage is due to the unevenness or degree of smoothness of the generated DC. With a fault in the alternator which causes loss of one of the three AC phases, or with an open rectifying diode which

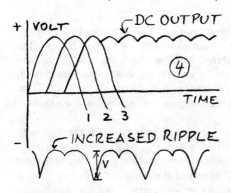

causes loss of one peak at plus or minus, additional "ripple" will be present in the generated direct current output.

Sketch ④ shows how normally three phases follow each other and produce closely spaced pulses of direct current. The very slight, rapid change in voltage is called ripple and is an alternating current component of the DC output : like AC superimposed on absolutely smooth DC . Directly underneath in the sketch is a voltage output curve with one peak missing. The much increased ripple voltage, the difference between peaks and valleys, can be measured on the AC scale of the Volt Ohm Meter (VOM). But you need a reference measurement for comparison, taken under similar conditions, with same battery capacity since batteries are great at smoothing ripples.

ROTOR TESTING

With the alternator disassembled, you test the rotor field coil for
continuity from one slip ring, through the coil winding, to the other
slip ring. With the VOM switched to Ohm, zero adjusted, touch the
test leads to the slip rings : one to each ring. The meter should read
about zero Ohm. Field coil resistances range from about 3 to 5 Ohm
and the usual Ohm meters cannot distinguish between a few Ohm and
zero Ohm.

Field coil and slip rings are insulated from the rotor shaft. Verify
this by touching one VOM test wire to a slip ring and the other test
wire to the rotor shaft : no electrical connection should have the meter
needle stay at the infinite Ohm end of the scale.

Much more important than these tests on the disassembled
alternator are tests of rotor and field coil which can be carried out
from the outside, as quick tests in trouble shooting. Many alternators
allow tests of the field coil without disassembly.

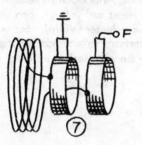

Alternators with external
regulators are almost always
the type P , with one brush
connected to ground, sketch ⑦.
The VOM should read zero Ohm
between the external field
terminal F (FIELD, F, FLD, DF)
and ground, or minus in alternators with isolated ground.

Even though you would get
the same reading if the field
winding or a slip ring were shorted, such trouble is rare because the
short would usually have high current flow for a moment which would
then melt a wire and cause an open (non conducting) field coil. Such
open field would give an infinite Ohm reading between field terminal
and ground.

To uncover the less likely problem of a shorted field (which would
have destroyed the regulator : check that), connect battery power,
plus 12 V for 12 Volt systems, through a 5 A or 10 A fuse to the field
terminal, regulator disconnected, alternator does not have to run. Only
if the fuse blows is the field shorted.

Alternators with internal or attached regulators often allow
regulator and brush assembly to be taken off from outside. We can then
touch the VOM test leads directly to the slip rings or, if the brushes
remain in place, to the brush terminals, proceeding as with external
regulator alternators.

EMERGENCY REPAIRS

This section will not touch on standard repairs which an alternator shop
would carry out and which normally consist of replacing faulty parts
with exact replacements, if not replacing the whole alternator. The
steps in this section are intended to help you put a faulty alternator or
regulator back into operation when there is no help from an alternator
shop and when replacement parts are not available either, but when
you are willing to try the slightly unusual instead of just giving up.

OPEN MAIN DIODE : If there is just one diode open, and none
shorted, best probably is to continue to operate the alternator. Its
output will be diminished, the voltage regulator will try to push it back
to the original output which will place greater than normal current
loads in the remaining, operating diodes. This in turn will produce
greater heat at these diodes : operate the alternator at highest possible
speed with greatest cooling air flow. Charge one battery at a time
instead of all in parallel if so equipped. See section on regulators,
consider reducing voltage setting or restricting field current.

SHORTED MAIN DIODE : Only one diode is open : disconnect
the AC wire from the tip of this diode. If you have a Delco type bridge
of diodes where individual diode terminals are not accessible,
disconnect the AC stator wire(s) which serve the shorted diode. This
will disable one AC phase with its plus and minus diodes. It will no
longer short all generated AC but will give reduced but useful output,
as with one open diode. Follow same operating precautions as in the
paragraph above.

SEVERAL OPEN OR SHORTED MAIN DIODES : if at least one plus
and one minus diode at the same AC terminal are still in tact, the
alternator should give some small output. The AC terminal (tip) of all
shorted diodes must be disconnected.
   A more involved repair depends on finding other diodes large enough
in Ampere rating to be of use : if you can find diodes from another
alternator, regardless whether it is a complete bridge assembly as in
Delco alternators, or separate plus and minus heat sinks with three
diodes each, you could mount them on a surface near the engine.
Connect three #12 stranded wires to the AC stator terminals inside the
alternator, solder the connections, run wires to the outside, lash them
securely away from rotor and other moving parts, connect to diodes at
any (almost) distance, and connect diodes to battery, sketch ① .
Since the diodes lack the normal forced air cooling, additional
aluminum sheet metal in contact with the heat sinks would help .

Extra heat sink sheet metal must consist of two separate pieces, one in good (thermal) contact with the plus fins, the other with the minus fins of the diode rectifyer bridge. A single solid piece would short plus to minus. CAUTION : heat sink is hot, live, voltage at AC and DC terminals, insulate, do not short : sparks, heat.

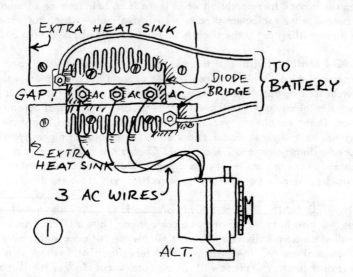

Finally, if that is the only remaining possibility, you may use the splitter or isolating diodes or charging diodes as rectifyers. See details about such diodes. Make wire connections to any two of the three stator AC terminals and run wires (insulated stranded # 12) to the outside of alternator, lash clear of rotor, connect one of the two wires to ground or battery minus, the other to the "Alternator" terminal of the splitter or charging diodes, their battery perminals remain as originally connected to battery plus. Not a very efficient arrangement but will produce some output charging current to battery. Wiring is shown in sketch ② .

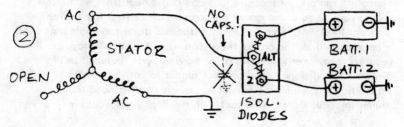

FAULTY DIODE TRIO : Single diodes number 1N5400 or 1N5401 can be used to replace a faulty diode in most diode trios. See section diodes. Solder parallel to open diode trio diode, or replace entire trio with three of the individual diodes and a few inches of wire. Source for the diodes : radio and electronic parts stores.

Or remove the faulty diode trio. Install a new wire from the engine key switch to the alternator auxiliary plus terminal. Pick the key switch terminal which is "hot" when key and engine are on. This

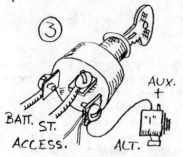

way, no electricity is waisted on field and regulator current when engine is off, because key switch also is off.

Connect to terminal "1" (Delco), D+ or "61" (Bosch, Marchal, Paris-Rhone), or "L" (Hitachi, Mitsubishi) terminal on alternator, sketch ③ .

If the alternator has an attached or external regulator, take wire off faulty plus aux. terminal and connect, with longer #14 or #16 wire to switched terminal of key switch.

FAULTY ISOLATING DIODE ON MOTOROLA : Compare with earlier explanation and diagram of this arrangement. If isolating diode is found open, damage to regulator is likely. If isolating diode is found shorted, you may continue to operate the alternator as usual

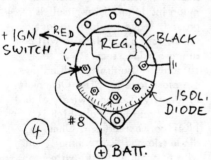

except that regulator and field current is being drained from the battery when the engine is off : a switch is necessary to prevent this.

However, a shorted isolating diode by itself would hardly be noticed. Make sure there is no other problem.

With an open isolating diode, reconnect wires as in sketch ④ .

Main output wire to REG terminal, wire from REG terminal to switched terminal on key switch.

FAULTY INTERNAL VOLTAGE REGULATOR : Applies to mostly
type N small to medium sized alternators. Delco internal regulators
are easy to replace, same regulator is used in very many different
alternator models. Since these alternators are in abundant use, you
may find a replacement even in remote places. See details in the
regulator section. In some other alternators in this group, regulators
are much more difficult to reach and replace, even if you had the
exact replacement (Hitachi, Mitsibishi).

    REGULATOR IS OPEN : no alternator output, regulator may
stay in place. Follow procedure to connect external field current
supply, see below.

    REGULATOR IS SHORTED : maximum alternator output, much
gassing in batteries, alternator gets hot . Regulator must be disconnected. In Delco, Hitachi, Mitsubishi alternators, disconnet regulator
terminal from minus brush. Leave diode trio in place .

CONNECT FIELD WIRE : to operate the alternator with an external
voltage regulator or other source of field current, we must make a
connection in the alternator since this group of alternators has no
outside field terminal. All have in common that this connection is
made to the minus brush, the
brush not connected to the diode
trio. All of these alternators are
type N .

Delco : connect wire to metal
tab at test hole, fasten wire under
small hex head screw which has
nylon insulator. Screw itself is
ground, leave insulator in tact,
see sketch ⑤ . Thin wire will do,
run to outside, secure it.

Hitachi, Mitsubishi : both brushes
are close together. Use Ohm meter
to identify. Connect wire (solder)
to that brush terminal which is
NOT connected (zero Ohm) to
diode trio and "L" terminal. Run
wire to outside, secure with
cable ties, keep clear of rotor.
Hitachi most models : sketch ⑥.

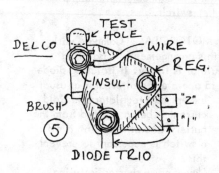

FAULTY ATTACHED VOLTAGE REGULATOR : With alternators which allow you to remove the attached regulator while leaving the brush holder in place (Motorola, Leece-Neville, Paris-Rhone, Marchal, but not Bosch), disconnect and remove the regulator. Use the VOM, Ohm range, zero adjusted, and measure between brush terminals, plus aux. termina, and minus (ground if minus is case).

TYPE N : none of the brushes is grounded, one of the brushes is in contact with the plus aux. terminal or diode trio terminal . Since the field coil has only about 3 to 5 Ohms resistance and connects both brushes with alternator assembled, both brushes will measure near zero Ohm between brush and plus aux. terminal. Try to see which of the two is on + aux. (D+, 61, REG). Connect a wire to the OTHER brush which will be the one with connection to the old regulator. Label this wire FIELD TYPE N .

TYPE P : one of the brushes is grounded, often through the metal brackets of the brush holder. The other brush has a connection to the regulator. Install a new wire to this brush terminal and label the wire FIELD TYPE P . You could use the Ohm meter to verify : both brushes show near zero Ohm to minus/ground. No connection to plus auxiliary terminal or diode trio .

Follow procedure to connect external regulator or other method to handle field current, below .

FAULTY EXTERNAL VOLTAGE REGULATOR : alternator will have a field terminal "F" at its outside which is connected by wire to the voltage regulator. Disconnect the faulty regulator and use the Ohm meter to identify your type of alternator, compare the section which explains types P and N .

TYPE P : near zero Ohm between F terminal and ground.

TYPE N : rare in this group . High or infinite Ohm between F terminal and ground. Plus supply is needed to the other brush .
TWO FIELD TERMINALS : if one is grounded, use the other as "F" and call alternator a type P .

Connect a wire to the field F terminal and label FIELD TYPE (N or P depending on your tests) .

STATUS : You have tested the alternator and connected a new field wire to it. You now need a source of field current to make the alternator generate output again. There are several possibilities :

FIELD CURRENT

EXTERNAL VOLTAGE REGULATOR : Should match voltage, that is, 12 V regulator for 12 V system, 24 V for 24 V system, et cetera. If at all possible, the replacement regulator should be the same type as the alternator : type P regulator for a type P alternator. If that cannot be found, a type P regulator can be made to work with a type N alternator but the other way around may be more complicated. Regulators can not normally be converted (P to N, N to P) but alternators can : instructions follow.

    If you get an obscure regulator without instructions, or if the usual instructions not clearly identify functions of terminals, test the regulator with a test light. See section on voltage regulators and use sketches there, to identify or at least tell brand and its usual letter or number identification of terminals. Try for the simplest, three terminal regulator. Note that the functions of more elaborate regulators, such as switching off when alternator stops, excite current, pilot charging light, can usually be added to a basic regulator.

    Sketch ① shows a 3-terminal Chrysler type P regulator hooked up to the field wire of a type P alternator. Before connecting to the alternator, it is prudent to connect a test light, in place of the field

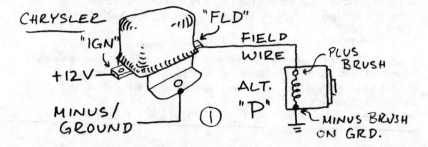

coil, to regulator and minus/ground, compare regulator tests. The light should be on brightly. Note that regulator bracket is ground. Connect plus terminal to key switch, so that power is off when engine off : avoids dead batteries from wasted field current. This type P regulator is solid state even though the housing suggests a mechanical version. To tell the difference : solid state has a single rivet head underneath, mechanical have one or two wire wound power resistors underneath.

Sketch ② shows a 3 – terminal Chrysler type N solid state regulator connected to the new field wire of a type N alternator。Before you connect the alternator, use a test light in place of the alternator field coil, between plus and regulator field terminal : light should be bright.

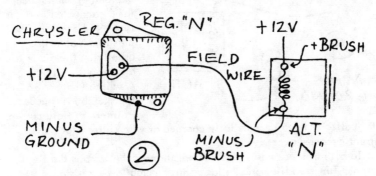

The regulator steel housing is ground, circuit is cast in, visible at back. Two terminals within triangular plastic socket can be soldered. Details of resgulators in that section. Other type N regulators can be used instead but bulk of these are more complicated or are made for installation inside alternator.

Note that the type N alternator requires plus 12 V connected to its plus brush or plus field terminal. Often, this source of 12 V is the diode trio or auxiliary plus terminal of the alternator : leave as it was originally connected if components are working. Otherwise, make a connection between switched key switch terminal and + brush, and connection key switch to regulator as sketched. This will switch off power when engine is off and key turned off, avoiding battery drain by field when the alternator is off.

UNREGULATED FIELD CURRENT : If no replacement regulator is available, alternator output can be generated with field current from a fixed or variable resistor or rheostat, or from electronic alternator controls. In our emergency, a lamp is likely the easiest to find.

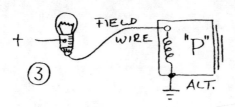

As in sketch ③ , the lamp is connected between plus (switch needed) and the field wire of the type P alternator. Output current of the alternator will depend on lamp wattage, alternator speed, battery size and state of charge, and several other factors. The light should have between 5 and 15 Watt, two or more smaller lamps may be connected in parallel. It is essential that you watch battery (overcharging) and alternator (excessive heat), see comments below.

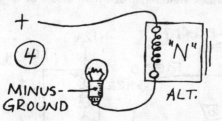

Sketch ④ shows such lamp connected to a type N alternator. The plus terminal will usually be the diode trio or plus aux. terminal. A switch (not shown in the sketch) is needed to interrupt field current after batteries have become fully charged or when alternator output current becomes excessive.

In both of these cases, the current through the lamp is the field current. Tungsten filaments in lamps have much lower resistance when cold than when hot and bright. A lamp with high wattage may not become bright but at the same time allow excessive field current.

If available, a resistor may also be used as an emergency regulator replacement. It is connected exactly like the lamps in sketched ③ or ④. A so called power resistor is necessary. With a value of 10 Ohm, and a field coil resistance of 4 Ohm, slightly under one Ampere of field current would flow at 13 Volt. The resistor should have a rating of 20 Watt or greater : it will get hot.

CAUTION : Alternator must be connected to its load, the battery, at all times. It otherwise can generate high output voltage, a shock hazard and risk to diodes and regulators. You must watch batteries to avoid overcharging which causes water from the electrolyte to be decomposed (gassing : explosive) and can overheat smaller batteries with high current. With large batteries, high alternator output current can overheat the alternator itself and associated wiring.

CONVERT ALTERNATOR FROM N TO P   : Relatively easy to do.
Note that in type N alternators, none of the two brushes or field
terminals are grounded. One brush is on plus aux. or diode trio, the
other is connected to the regulator. To convert to type P, disconnect
both brushes, reconnect one to ground, connect a wire to the other
brush, lead outside, label FIELD TYPE P .
        The diode trio or auxiliary plus terminal can still be used :
connect it by wire to outside, use it as the plus supply for regulator or
charge indicator ("idiot") light.

CONVERT ALTERNATOR FROM P TO N : Much more difficult,
only because one of the two brushes in the type P alternator is grounded
which is often done through the hardware of the brush holder and not
easy to isolate from ground. If you see a way to do that, possibly after
taking the brush holder out to inspect, the rest is easy. With both
brushes isolated, connect one to plus (wire to key switch outside, or
inside to diode trio or auxiliary plus terminal if available), the other
brush gets a wire to the outside, with label FIELD TYPE N . You must
use an outside regulator, type N, or other temporary control of field
current between this wire and ground.

MANUAL ALTERNATOR CONTROLS WITH REGULATOR : There is
at least one manual alternator control on the market which incorporates
a type N voltage regulator. All it requires is alternator which may or
may not have a working regulator. The control allows selection by
hand of alternator output current, switches hand selected field current
off when batteries reach full charge and switches to its own voltage
regulator which then runs the alternator like other regulators and
alternators.

ADD EXCITE CURRENT : If the engine must be revved up after
starting, before the ammeter will show any alternator output current,
the alternator may need excitation, or more of it (Not excitement :
balloons and floor show probably wont' do) . The alternator will be
one with auxiliary plus terminal, diode trio or isolating diode which
supply field current. To cure, connect a resistor (50 Ohm , 5 Watt)
between switched key terminal (plus only when key is turned on) and
the auxiliary plus terminal, whether it is by diode trio or isolating
diode. Or install a charge pilot light, see next .

ADD A CHARGE INDICATOR "IDIOT" LIGHT : Can serve to
feed excite current, see previous paragraph and section earlier in the
book. The light is connected between switched key switch terminal
(plus on only when key switched on) and the auxiliary plus terminal.
In some alternators , especially type N, a resistor may be necessary
between the diode trio plus terminal and ground, to allow enough
current to flow through the light to ground to create enough brightness.
Such resistor can be seen fastened between two of the three screws
which hold the flat plastic internal regulator in Delco alternators.
A resistor of 100 Ohm, 2 Watt will do for small lamps to one Watt,
lower resistance values with up to 5 Watt for larger lamps, all this
for 12 Volt systems .

ADD A TACHOMETER TERMINAL : Especially on diesel engines,
tachometers are often operated with the changing frequency of the
alternator's alternating current. Many alternators have stator AC
terminals which serve the purpose and are called R , W, N, STA, or
TACH. Connection to any of the three AC stator terminals is otherwise
necessary. You can avoid opening the alternator if the tip of one of
the three plus rectifying diodes can be reached through one of the
vent holes at the back housing : solder another thin wire to the solder
joint which now connects a stator wire to that diode, leaving the
stator wire well connected.

Main dimensions in inches, within about ± one eighth inch, given with
letter code with following sketches, to make identification and replacement with other models and brands easier. Since pulleys must line up,
note that lengths and bracket setbacks are measured from center of
pulley groove.

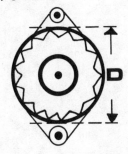

D diameter of main body or stator, less
brackets, through bolt bosses

L length from center of pulley groove,
includes integral, attached regulator
but not studs, terminals, capacitors.

R radius, shaft axis to mounting bolt
axis. For some alternators, angle to the
tension bracket hole is shown, viewed
when looking on to pulley.

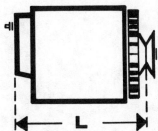

A setback from center of pulley
groove to face of mounting bracket.
Use to check if new alternator will
line up in existing bracket.

B length of single, so called spool
mount bracket.

C clearance between dual brackets.

E thickness of front bracket.

F thickness of rear bracket : often has
sliding bushing longer than F .

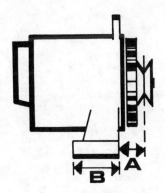

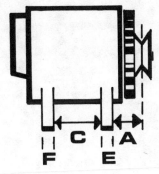

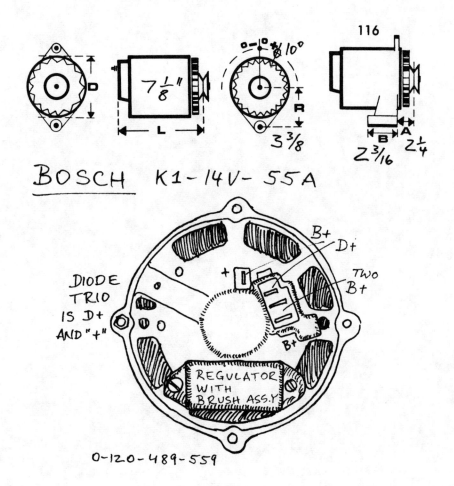

BOSCH K1-14V-55A

116

7 1/8"

L

3 3/8

⌀10°

R

B   A

2 3/16   2 1/4

DIODE
TRIO
IS D+
AND "+"

B+
D+

TWO
B+

B+

REGULATOR
WITH
BRUSH ASS.Y

0-120-489-559

DIODE TRIO TO D+, "+" IN RECT.
HOLE, AND TO METAL FINGER
UNDER REGULATOR.

REGULATOR WITH BRUSH ASSEMBLY,
SIMILAR TO OTHER BOSCH ALT.,
EASY TO CHECK/REPLACE.

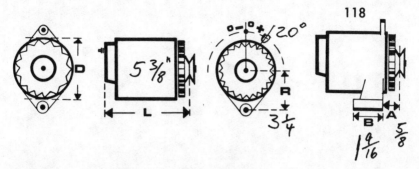

BOSCH K1-14V-55A

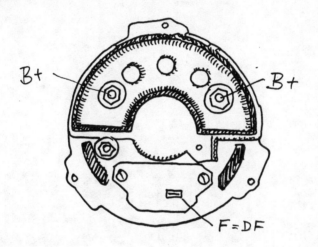

B+   B+

F=DF

0-120-400-757

DIODE TRIO TO 61/D+. EXTERNAL
REGULATOR CONNECTS TO 61/D+,
D-, DF = POS. BRUSH.

REMOVABLE BRUSH HOLDER ASS.Y

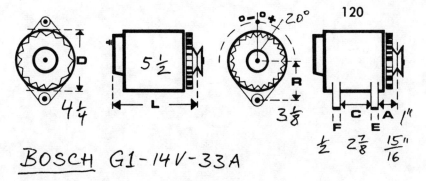

BOSCH G1-14V-33A

EXT. REG.

DIODE TRIO

0-120-300
-569

B+

D+

B+

B+

SHOWN WITH BRUSH ASSEMBLY
REMOVED:
DIODE TRIO TO D+
AND METAL FINGER
UNDER BRUSH ASS.Y.
INNER BRUSH GROUNDED,
OUTER ON "DF".

BRUSH

D-

DF

D+

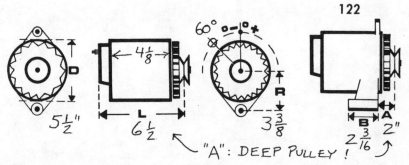

60°

"A": DEEP PULLEY!

$5\frac{1}{2}$"

$4\frac{1}{8}$

L

$6\frac{1}{2}$

R

$3\frac{3}{8}$

B $2\frac{3}{16}$

A 2"

BOSCH K1-14V-65A

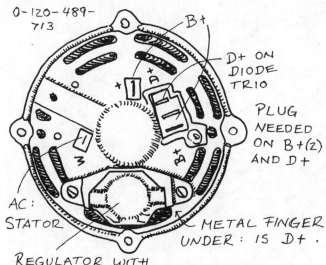

0-120-489-713

B+

D+ ON DIODE TRIO

PLUG NEEDED ON B+(2) AND D+

METAL FINGER UNDER: IS D+.

AC: STATOR

REGULATOR WITH BRUSH ASSEMBLY, REMOVEABLE.

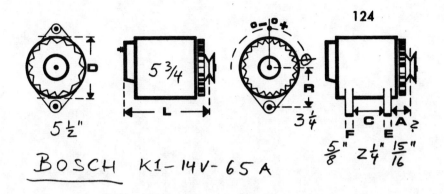

$5\frac{1}{2}''$ $5\frac{3}{4}$ $3\frac{1}{4}$ $\frac{5}{8}''$ $2\frac{1}{4}''$ $\frac{15}{16}''$

BOSCH K1-14V-65A

0-120-489-874

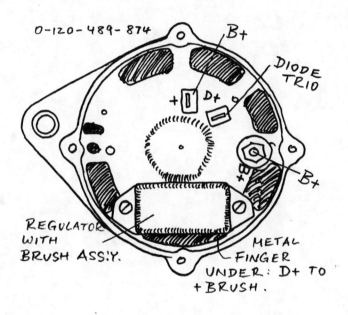

B+

DIODE TRIO

D+

B+

B+

REGULATOR WITH BRUSH ASS'Y.

METAL FINGER UNDER: D+ TO +BRUSH.

DELCO - REMY

Model numbers with some specifications (negative, isolated, or positive ground, 12 V, 24 V, 32 V, max. field current, output current, RPM) are listed together with SERIES and TYPE numbers in Bulletin 1G-188. The current issue (3/85) lists over 900 alternator models.

Model numbers consist of seven digits, usually stamped into front housing, followed by Ampere rating (example : 1105171 63A). SERIES and TYPE numbers are used to group alternators by size and features. Increasing series numbers (example 10 SI, 15 SI, 20 SI) go with increasing physical size and current ratings while type numbers (example : 100, 116, 200, 300) indicate features such as bearings, shaft size, type of cooling (air or engine oil). Type numbers increase with durability.

DELCOTRON Alternators by Series and Type (1978 - 1985)

10 SI - 100 : internal IC regulator, ball bearing at front, external fan, excited through terminal "1", battery voltage sensed through terminal "2" which permanently connected to battery (drain is low). Current ratings (all 12 Volt except where noted, all negative ground except where noted) : 37 A, 42 A, 55 A, 63 A.

10 SI - 102 : similar, 16 A, 18 A, 21 A, 24V-18 A, 24V-21A.

10 SI - 110 : similar, 37 A, 42 A.

10 SI - 116 : similar, 40 A, 42 A, 61 A, 63 A, 24V-40 A.

10 SI - 136 : similar, 40 A, 61 A, 63 A, 72 A, 24V-40 A.

12 SI - 100 : similar, 56 A, 66 A, 78 A, 94 A.

15 SI - 100 : similar, 56 A, 70 A, 85 A.

15 SI - 116 : similar, 85 A, 105 A .

17 SI - 100 : 94 A, 97 A, 108 A, 120 A.

20 SI - 300 : for high durability, heavy bearings each end, heavy belt load, medium current ratings, brushless (stationary field coil), self-exciting by residual magnetism, internal IC regulator has no terminals to outside ("2" sense terminal internally on BAT), some have "R" terminal for accessory switching. 60 A, 24V-35 A, 24V-45A .

29 SI – 300 : very similar to 20 SI – 300 but output 90A .

25 SI – 400 : extra long life, brushless as 20 SI and 29 SI, solid state internal regulator with discrete components and screwdriver voltage adjustment, individual field diodes (diode trio) on same PC board, accessible under large flat lid over back housing, 75 A, 75 A positive ground.

25 SI – 440 : similar, 24V–50 A.

25 SI – 450 : similar, battery disconnect with engine running does not damage regulator or diodes, 75 A, 24V–50 A, 24V–75 A.

27 SI – 100 : similar to 10 SI, 12 SI, 15 SI series. 80 A, 100 A, 120 A.

27 SI – 200 : large front ball bearing for heavier belt loads, similar to 20 SI except has external voltage adjustment square plug, see sketch. Excited by residual magnetism, no external regulator terminals but has "R" terminal, 65 A, 80 A, 100 A, 24V–65 A, 65 A positive ground.

27 SI – 205 : similar, 65 A, 80 A, 100 A.   27 SI – 202 : 24V–30 A.

30 SI – 400 : brushless, electrically like 20 SI but with external voltage adjustment plug like 27 SI – 200, has diode trio similar to 10 SI, 12 SI, 15 SI alternators, also similar main diode bridge ass'y, accessible under flat lid over back housing, 90 A, 90 A positive grd.

30 SI – 450 : similar, 24V–60 A, 32V–60 A, both with isolated ground.

30 SI/TR series : same as 30 SI, with added transformer and rectifying diode bridge, has 12 V and 24 V output, common case ground terminal and "R".

31 SI – 500 : 85 A, 135 A, 24V–75 A. 31 SI – 550 : 24V–75 A.

32 SI – 600 : brushless, direct driven, no belt or pulley, engine oil cooled and lubricated, electrically similar to 30 SI but with discrete component regulator, voltage screwdriver adjustment, 85 A, 24V–85 A.

40 SI – 150 : heavy bearings and high output, diode trio with AC wire terminals, two or three main rectifying diode bridges in parallel, accessible under flat rear cover, voltage adjustment plug. Not listed in current model number bulletin.

10 DN-100, 112...

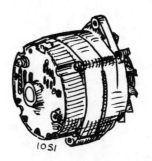

10SI

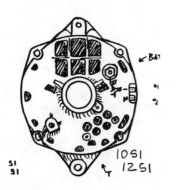

SI
SI

10SI
12SI

← BAT

BAT 1 2

R T

15SI
17SI

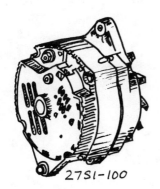

27SI-100

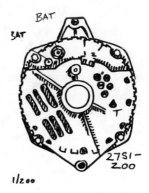

BAT

3AT

27SI-200

1/200

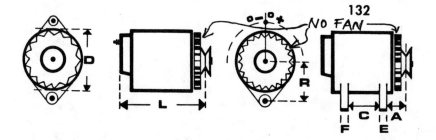

DELCO-REMY

20 DN - 100 AND 150
(1962)
EXT. REG.

SERVICE
BULLETIN
No. IG·271
(1963)

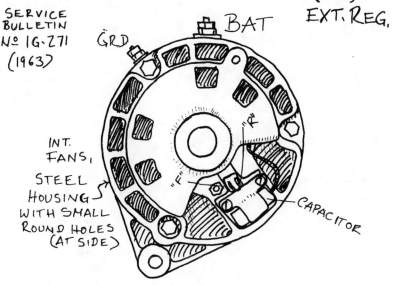

INT.
FANS,
STEEL
HOUSING
WITH SMALL
ROUND HOLES
(AT SIDE)

REMOVEABLE
BRUSH HOLDER, WITH "F" AND "R"
TERMINAL SPADE LUGS.
TO RE-INSTALL: PIN HOLE: HOLD BACK
BRUSHES WITH PIN.

CAN BE USED + OR - GRD: JUMPER
WIRE INSIDE CONNECTS + OR - TO CASE.

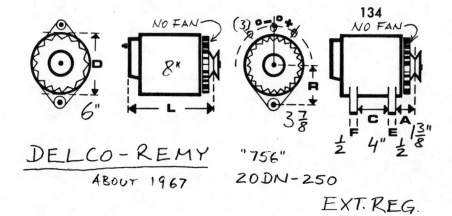

NO FAN

(3)

134
NO FAN

D

6"

8^x

L

R

$3\frac{7}{8}$

C   A

F   E

$\frac{1}{2}$ 4" $\frac{1}{2}$ $1\frac{3}{8}$"

DELCO - REMY

ABOUT 1967

"756"

20DN - 250

EXT. REG.

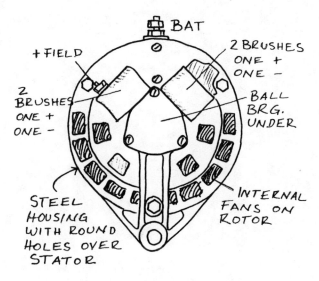

BAT

+ FIELD

2 BRUSHES
ONE +
ONE -

2
BRUSHES
ONE +
ONE -

BALL
BRG.
UNDER

STEEL
HOUSING
WITH ROUND
HOLES OVER
STATOR

INTERNAL
FANS ON
ROTOR

TWO BRUSH HOLDERS, EASY TO
REMOVE. EACH HAS TWO BRUSHES,
IN PARALLEL, BY WIRES.

SERVICE BULLETIN № 1G-27Z (1967)

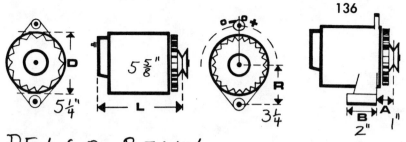

136

DELCO-REMY
DELCOTRON 10 DN-100, 112, 130, OR 133
SPADE LUGS PARALLEL: EXT. REG.

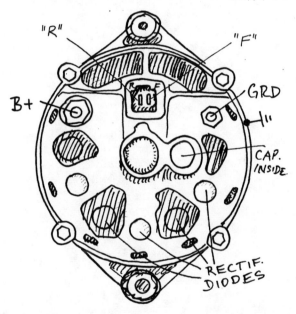

"R" "F"

B+ GRD
|1"

CAP. INSIDE

RECTIF. DIODES

SINCE ABOUT 1960. NOTE DIODES
PRESS FITTED INTO HOUSING AND HEAT
SINK. DIFFERENT FROM MOST CURRENT
MODELS. LARGE U-SHAPED HEAT SINK.
(SEE SKETCH OF MORE RECENT DIODE BRIDGE)

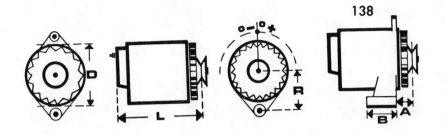

DELCO-REMY   15 SI—
                 17 SI—

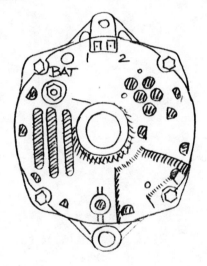

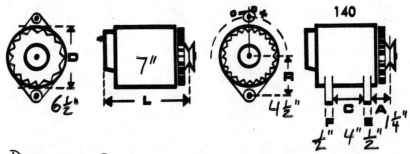

140

$\frac{1}{2}"$ 4" $\frac{1}{2}"$ $1\frac{1}{4}"$

DELCO-REMY

27 SI-200

INT. REG.

12V-65A

SOME WITH
DUAL
PULLEYS.

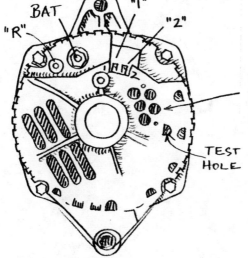

BAT

"R"

"1"

"2"

SOME WITH
LONG OVAL
VENT HOLES
HERE.

TEST
HOLE

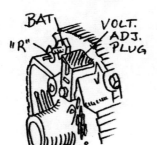

BAT

"R"

VOLT.
ADJ.
PLUG

MODELS WITH VOLTAGE
ADJUSTMENT: SQUARE
PLUG AND BRACKET
MOUNTED OVER "1" & "2"
TERMINALS.
(NUMBERS STILL
VISIBLE !)

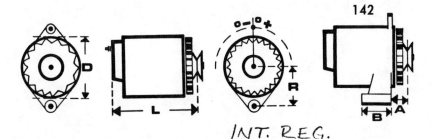

142

DELCO-REMY

INT. REG.

10 SI - 110 W. SCREEN

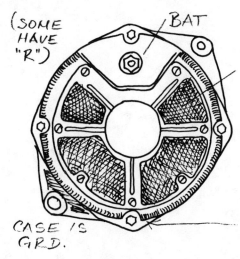

(SOME HAVE "R")

BAT

FINE MESH METAL SCREEN

FLAME-
DAMPENING SCREEN AND COVER HELD BY TROUGH BOLTS.

CASE IS GRD.

(ALSO HAS SCREEN IN FRONT HOUSING OPENINGS)

NO OUTSIDE "1" OR "2" TERMINALS.
DIODE TRIO CONNECTED TO "1" AND "2".

(SOME HAVE OVAL HOLE OVER "1" AND "2"
LUG TERMINALS, RUBBER PLUG ON "1" & "2")

DELCO-REMY SERVICE BULLETIN 1G-267 (1969)
                                  1G-278 (1980)

DELCO-REMY

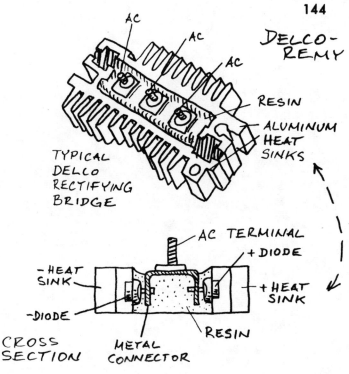

AC
AC
AC

RESIN

ALUMINUM
HEAT
SINKS

TYPICAL
DELCO
RECTIFYING
BRIDGE

AC TERMINAL

+ DIODE

+ HEAT
SINK

— HEAT
SINK

— DIODE

RESIN

METAL
CONNECTOR

CROSS
SECTION

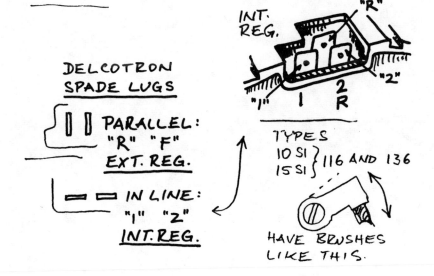

INT.
REG.

"R"

"2"

"1"

1
2
R

DELCOTRON
SPADE LUGS

PARALLEL:
"R" "F"
EXT. REG.

IN LINE:
"1" "2"
INT. REG.

TYPES
10 SI
15 SI } 116 AND 136

HAVE BRUSHES
LIKE THIS.

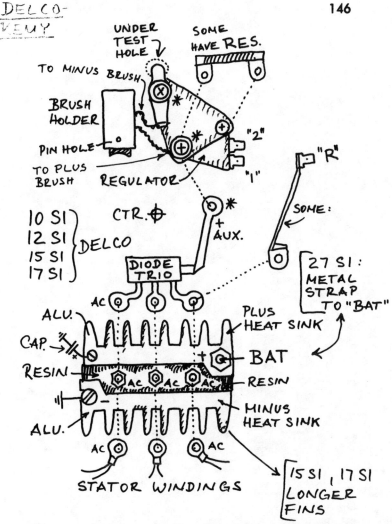

DELCO-REMY

UNDER TEST HOLE

SOME HAVE RES.

TO MINUS BRUSH

BRUSH HOLDER

PIN HOLE

TO PLUS BRUSH

REGULATOR

"2"

"1"

"R"

SOME:

10 SI
12 SI } DELCO
15 SI
17 SI

CTR.

* + AUX.

DIODE TRIO

27 SI: METAL STRAP TO "BAT"

AC

ALU.

CAP.

RESIN

ALU.

PLUS HEAT SINK

BAT

AC   AC   AC

RESIN

MINUS HEAT SINK

AC   AC

AC   AC

STATOR WINDINGS

15 SI , 17 SI LONGER FINS

DOTTED LINES SHOW HOW PARTS ARE
CONNECTED TO EACH OTHER. VIEWED
INTO INSIDE OF BACK HOUSING.
* NOTE INSULATION WASHERS: SCREWS
ARE GROUNDED, LUGS ARE INSULATED!

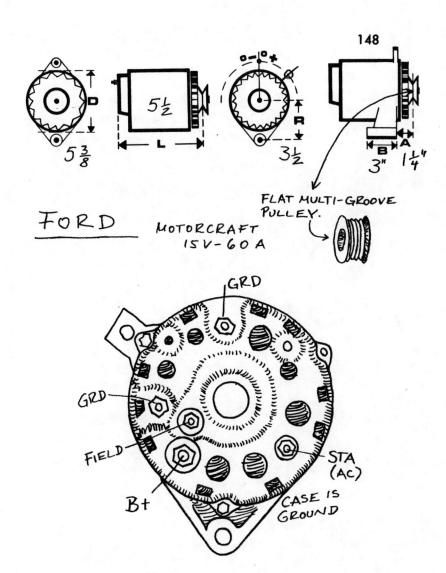

FLAT MULTI-GROOVE
PULLEY.

FORD   MOTORCRAFT
15V-60A

GRD

GRD

FIELD

Bt

STA
(AC)

CASE IS
GROUND

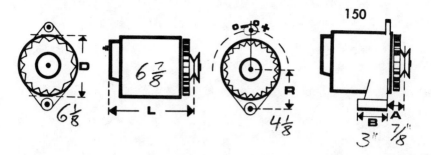

FORD

15V-65A
"AUTOLITE"

EXT. REG.

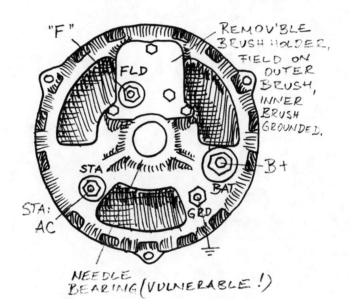

"F"

FLD

REMOV'BLE
BRUSH HOLDER,
FIELD ON
OUTER
BRUSH,
INNER
BRUSH
GROUNDED.

STA

B+

BAT

STA:
AC

GRD

NEEDLE
BEARING (VULNERABLE!)

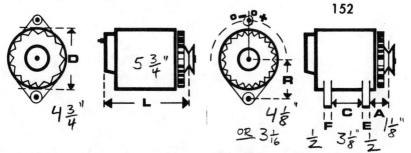

HITACHI   LT135-13B
14V-35A   EXT. REG. *

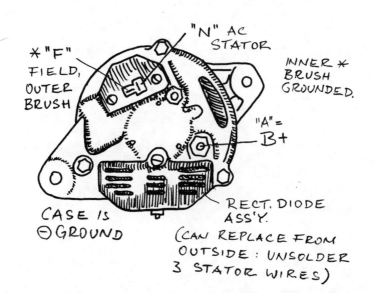

"N" AC STATOR

* "F" FIELD, OUTER BRUSH

INNER * BRUSH GROUNDED.

"A" = B+

CASE IS ⊖ GROUND

RECT. DIODE ASS'Y.

(CAN REPLACE FROM OUTSIDE: UNSOLDER 3 STATOR WIRES)

REMOVEABLE BRUSH HOLDER, MUST TAKE OUT BEFORE RE-ASSEMBLING ROTOR AND HOUSINGS (NO BRUSH HOLD-BACK PIN HOLE)

* SOME LOOK-ALIKES WITH ADDED INT. REG. AND DIODE TRIO, ARE TYPE N, STILL HAVE "F" AND "N" !

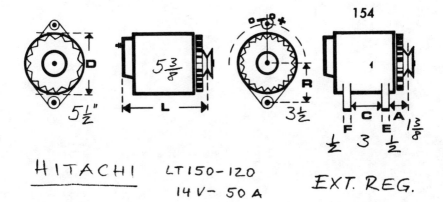

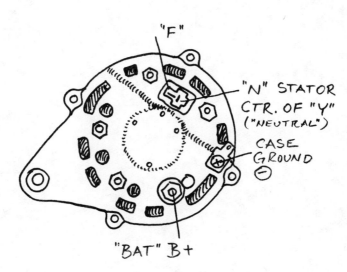

$5\frac{1}{2}$" $5\frac{3}{8}$ L $3\frac{1}{2}$ R

F $\frac{1}{2}$ 3 E $\frac{1}{2}$ A $1\frac{3}{8}$ C

<u>HITACHI</u>   LT150-120
                14V - 50 A   EXT. REG.

"F"

"N" STATOR
CTR. OF "Y"
("NEUTRAL")

CASE
GROUND
⊖

"BAT" B+

INNER BRUSH ON CASE - GROUND
OUTER BRUSH "F". NO DIODE TRIO.

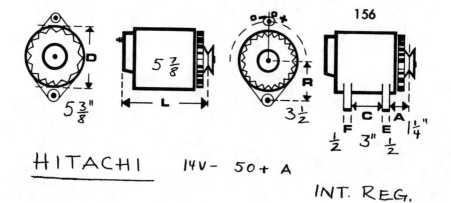

156

HITACHI   14V- 50+ A

INT. REG.

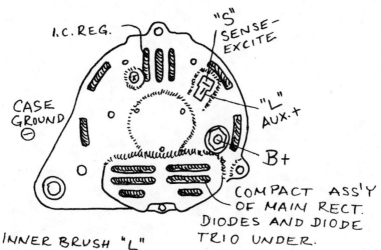

I.C. REG.

"S" SENSE-EXCITE

CASE GROUND

"L" AUX. +

B+

INNER BRUSH "L" AND DIODE TRIO. OUTER BRUSH ON REG.

COMPACT ASS'Y OF MAIN RECT. DIODES AND DIODE TRIO UNDER.

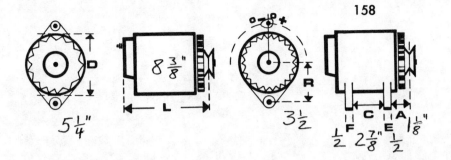

$5\frac{1}{4}"$ $8\frac{3}{8}"$ L $3\frac{1}{2}$ R   C   A $\frac{1}{8}"$ F   E $\frac{1}{2}$ $2\frac{7}{8}"$ $\frac{1}{2}$

HITACHI   LR-150-125B   14V-50A
            LR-160-74   14V-60A

INT. REG.

DIODE
   TRIO

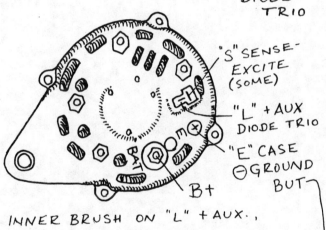

"S" SENSE-
   EXCITE
   (SOME)

"L" + AUX
DIODE TRIO

"E" CASE
⊖ GROUND
      BUT

B+

INNER BRUSH ON "L" + AUX.,
OUTER BRUSH ON REG.

TYPE "N"

MODEL L155-20: 55A
   "E" ISOL. GROUND, INT. REG.
   TYPE "N".

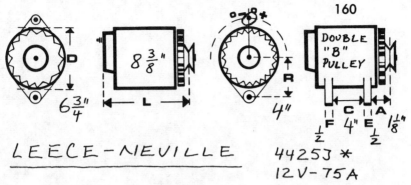

LEECE-NEVILLE

44253 *
12V - 75A

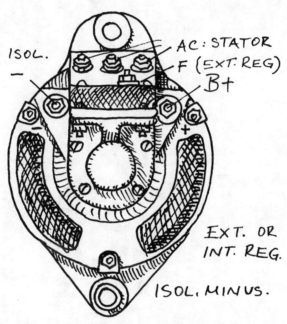

ISOL.

AC: STATOR
F (EXT. REG)
B+

EXT. OR
INT. REG.

ISOL. MINUS.

* 12V :   105 A IS 46253; 130A 47253
24V :   65 A IS 44263; 100A 46263
32V :   115 A IS 46323.

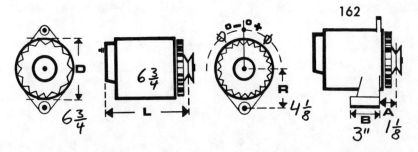

162

LEECE-NEVILLE

7014A 12V 65A *
EXT. REG *

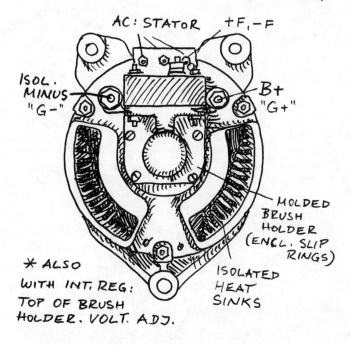

AC: STATOR   +F, -F

ISOL.
MINUS
"G-"

B+
"G+"

MOLDED
BRUSH
HOLDER
(ENCL. SLIP
RINGS)

* ALSO
WITH INT. REG:
TOP OF BRUSH
HOLDER. VOLT. ADJ.

ISOLATED
HEAT
SINKS

* 12 Volt : 105A 7600J, 130A 7700J, others.
  24 Volt : 60A 7509J, 85A 7512J.

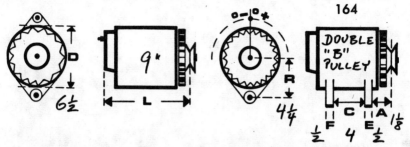

LEECE-NEVILLE   2300/2500/2600 J *

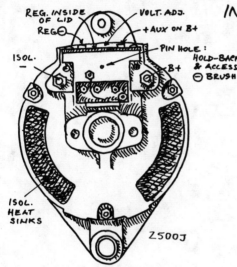

REG. INSIDE OF LID REG ⊖

VOLT. ADJ.

+ AUX ON B+

PIN HOLE: HOLD-BACK & ACCESS ⊖ BRUSH

ISOL.

B+

ISOL. HEAT SINKS

2500J

INT. REG.

(INSIDE OF FLAT PLATE, OVER BRUSH ASSEMBLY)

ALSO MADE W. EXT. REG.

DOUBLE "B" PULLEY

* 12 Volt : 65 A is 2300J, 75A 2360J, 90A 2500J, 105A 2600J,
    130A 2700J, 145A 2805J, 160A 2800J;
  24 Volt : 20A 2301J, 45A 2303J, 60A 2509J, 65A 2304J,
    85A 2511J;
  32 Volt : 60A 2302J .

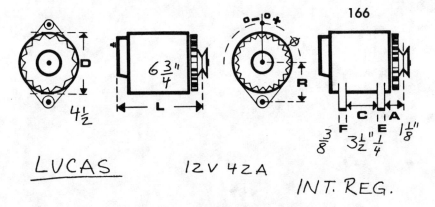

LUCAS 12V 42A INT. REG.

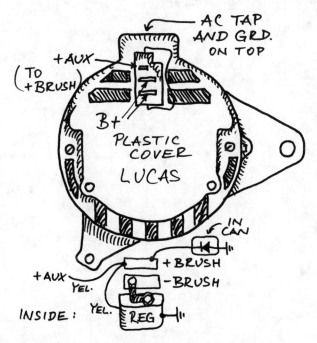

PLASTIC COVER OVER BACK : ACCESS
TO BRUSH TERM'LS AND REG : SMALL
ALU. CAN, HOUSING = GROUND.
NEEDS PLUG : TWO BIG SPADE LUGS B+.

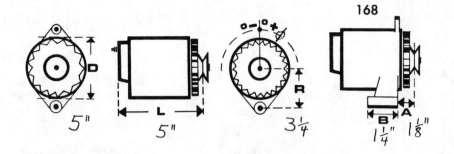

5" 5" 3¼ B 1¼" A 1⅛"

S.E.V. MARCHAL   EXT. REG.

14V – 60A

VOLVO PART № 5001655

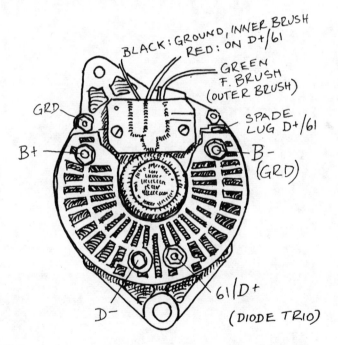

BLACK; GROUND, INNER BRUSH
RED; ON D+/61

GREEN
F. BRUSH
(OUTER BRUSH)

GRD

B+

SPADE
LUG D+/61

B –
(GRD)

61/D+

D –

(DIODE TRIO)

BLACK PLASTIC COVER. REMOVEABLE
BRUSH HOLDER, BLACK INNER BRUSH GRD.,
GREEN OUTER BRUSH + FIELD.
SIMILAR ALT. WITH ATTACHED REG (P. 76: ㉟)

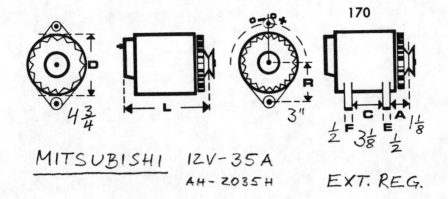

170

MITSUBISHI 12V-35A

AH-2035H

EXT. REG.

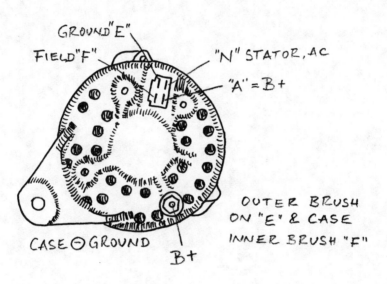

GROUND "E"

FIELD "F"

"N" STATOR, AC

"A" = B+

CASE ⊖ GROUND

B+

OUTER BRUSH
ON "E" & CASE
INNER BRUSH "F"

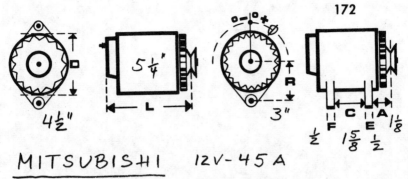

MITSUBISHI   12V-45A

A5T-15171

INT. REG
DIODE TRIO

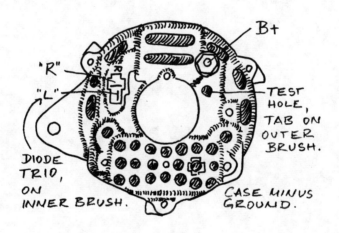

B+

"R"

"L"

TEST HOLE, TAB ON OUTER BRUSH.

DIODE TRIO, ON INNER BRUSH.

CASE MINUS GROUND.

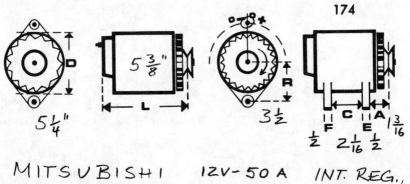

MITSUBISHI   12V-50A   INT. REG.,
               A2T-25271   DIODE
                            TRIO

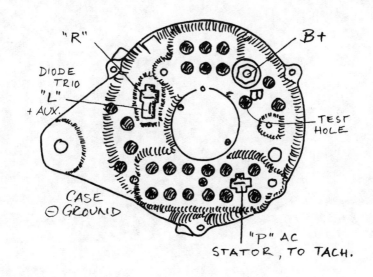

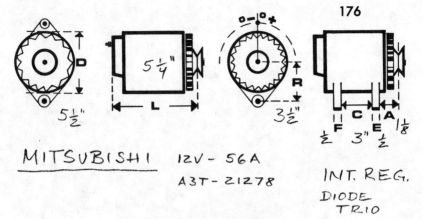

MITSUBISHI 12V – 56A

A3T – 21278

INT. REG.
DIODE
TRIO

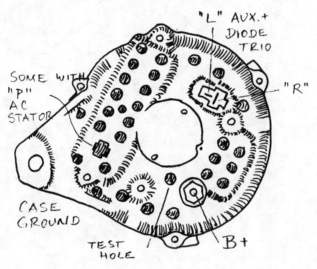

"L" AUX.+
DIODE
TRIO

"R"

SOME WITH
"P"
AC
STATOR

CASE
GROUND

TEST
HOLE

B+

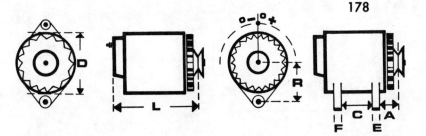

MITSUBISHI
12V - 65A INT. REG., PLUG:"R" AC, "L" + AUX.
D= 5½", L= 5½", R= 3½", F= ½, C= 2$\frac{1}{16}$, E= ½, A= 1$\frac{3}{16}$

12V - 45A INT. REG., PLUG:"R" AC, "L" + AUX.
D= 5, L= 5, R= 3, F= ½, C= 1$\frac{7}{8}$, E= ½, A= 1$\frac{1}{4}$

12V - 50A EXT. REG. AH-2250M
D= 5$\frac{1}{4}$", L= 5$\frac{1}{2}$", R= 3$\frac{1}{2}$", F= $\frac{1}{2}$", C= 2",
E= $\frac{1}{2}$", A= 1$\frac{1}{8}$".

MOTOROLA

Slip rings in most alternators outside of rear bearing : easy
access. Brush holders (see sketches on following pages)
located under a cover or under attached or flush mounted
or recessed regulator. Cover sometimes has shape of a
regulator but is not. Brush holders can be removed, replaced
without need to disassemble the alternator.

Models up to and including 55 Amp often have isolating diode
at back, see sketches : easy to recognize. Some larger
alternators are made with isolating diode which then is a
casting (instead of normal formed flat stock) with three press
fitted diodes in parallel.

Alternator model numbers consist of numbers and letters, some
beginning with "8" (US made) or "9" (made in France).
Smaller units for light/medium duty include groups with
A, MA, MH (heavy duty version of MA), 8AL, 8MA, 8MH,
MR (MA version with attached regulator), 8MR (similar), and
9 series.
HC is heavy duty version of MR.
Heavy duty (bearings) and higher output alternators have
designations with HA, MH, SA and 8SA (high output cast iron
housing), 8HA, 8MH, 8SB (brushless, low cut in RPM, high
output rating), TA and 8TA (totally enclosed, housings with
cooling fins).
Load Handler (Motorola trademark) series 8LHA (84 A to
130 A output), 8LHC (160 A output).
Other models include series RA, 8AR, 8HC (marine, with
attached regulator), and UL listed marine alternators in the
MA, MR, 8MA, 8MR, and YSB series.
Many alternators without regulators (for external regulator) can
be retrofitted with attached regulators.

NOTE : Voltage regulator model numbers usually begin
with 8RG, 8RF, 8RH, 8RD , 9RC followed by usually four
digits . They are sometimes taken by mistake as the alternator
model number.

A letter following the four digits in alternator model numbers
sometimes identifies output rating : F (32 A, 35 A, 37 A),
G (40 A), K (51 A, 55 A), L (62 A), N (68 A), P (72 A),
R (84 A, 85 A, 90 A), V (130 A) .

MOTOROLA ISOLATING DIODES

ALWAYS AT OUTSIDE OF REAR
HOUSING : EASY TO IDENTIFY.

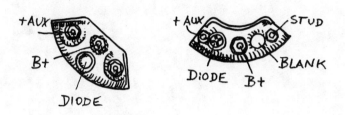

+AUX
B+
DIODE

+ AUX
STUD
DIODE
B+
BLANK

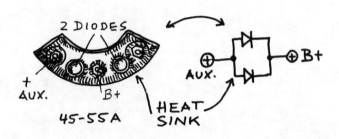

2 DIODES
+ AUX.
B+
45-55A
HEAT SINK
AUX.
⊕ B+

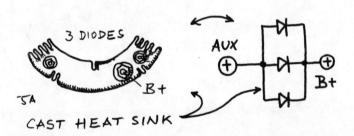

3 DIODES
5A
B+
CAST HEAT SINK
AUX
⊕
B+
⊕

NOTE: THE + AUX = "REG" TERMINAL
ON ALT. WITH ISOL. DIODE(S) IS
ABOUT 1 VOLT HIGHER THAN BATT.
VOLTAGE. AFFECTS REGULATORS !

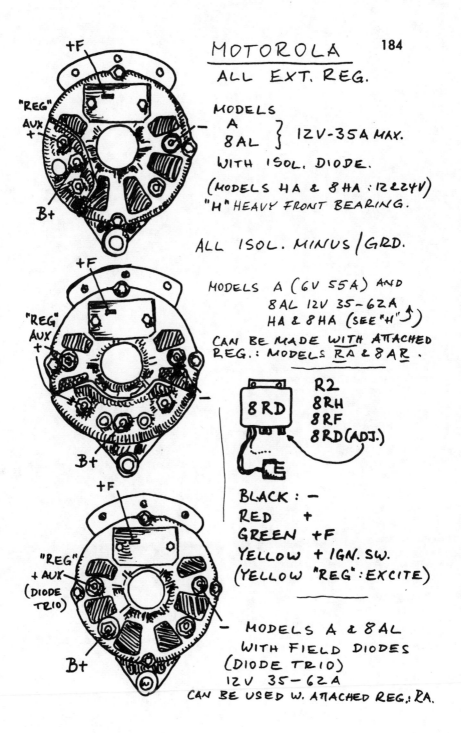

MOTOROLA

ALL EXT. REG.

MODELS
A
8AL } 12V-35A MAX.
WITH ISOL. DIODE.
(MODELS HA & 8HA : 12 & 24V)
"H" HEAVY FRONT BEARING.

ALL ISOL. MINUS/GRD.

MODELS A (6V 55A) AND
8AL 12V 35-62A
HA & 8HA (SEE "H")
CAN BE MADE WITH ATTACHED
REG.: MODELS RA & 8AR.

R2
8RD   8RH
          8RF
          8RD (ADJ.)

BLACK : −
RED   +
GREEN +F
YELLOW + IGN. SW.
(YELLOW "REG" : EXCITE)

− MODELS A & 8AL
    WITH FIELD DIODES
    (DIODE TRIO)
    12V 35-62A
CAN BE USED W. ATTACHED REG.: RA.

Labels on diagrams:

+F
"REG"
AUX
+
B+

+F
"REG"
AUX
+
B+

+F
"REG"
+ AUX
(DIODE TRIO)
B+

MOTOROLA : SIMILAR ON ALL.

ONE :

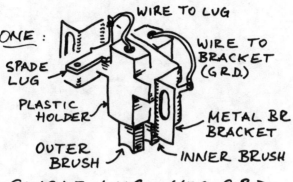

WIRE TO LUG

WIRE TO BRACKET (GRD.)

SPADE LUG

PLASTIC HOLDER

METAL BR BRACKET

OUTER BRUSH

INNER BRUSH

SINGLE LUG : NEG. GRD.

TWO :

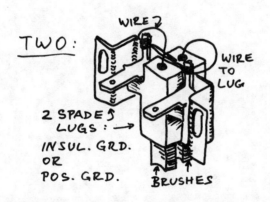

WIRE ?

WIRE TO LUG

2 SPADE LUGS : →

INSUL. GRD.
OR
POS. GRD.

BRUSHES

MOTOROLA REG. WITH TWO FIELD WIRES

(GREEN, SPADE LUGS, UNDER REG.)
SEE SECTION ON VOLT. REG.: "N".

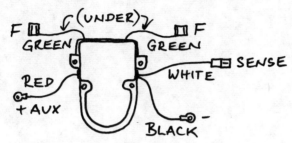

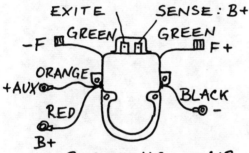

REG. ON HC AND MR

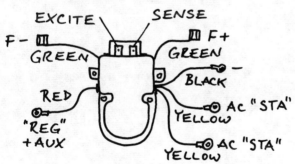

REG. ON 8MR: TYPE "N".

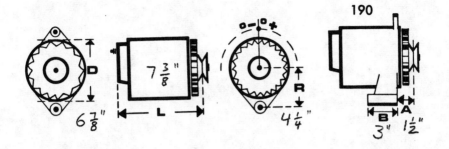

190

MOTOROLA

12V 84A

* DIODES IN
  HOUSING: MUST
REMAIN POS. GRD. OR
NEG. GRD. AS BUILT!
(8 LHA 2011 SHOWN)

8 LHA 2011 R NEG. GRD.
8 LHA 2012 R POS. GRD.

INT. (ATTACHED) REG.

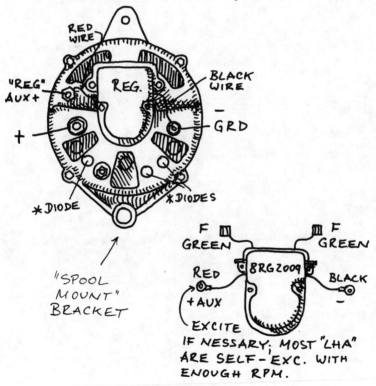

RED WIRE

"REG" AUX +

REG.

BLACK WIRE

— GRD

+

* DIODE   * DIODES

"SPOOL MOUNT" BRACKET

F GREEN   F GREEN

RED   8RG2009   BLACK

+ AUX   —

EXCITE
IF NESSARY: MOST "LHA"
ARE SELF-EXC. WITH
ENOUGH RPM.

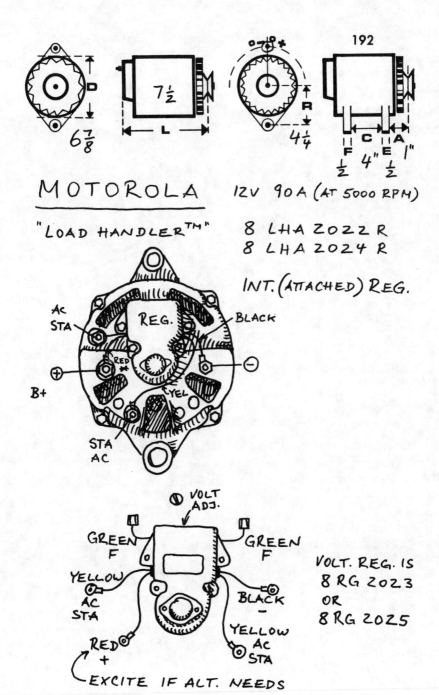

192

D

$7\frac{1}{2}$

L

$6\frac{7}{8}$

R

$4\frac{1}{4}$

F $\frac{1}{2}$ C 4"   E $\frac{1}{2}$ A 1"

MOTOROLA

12V 90A (AT 5000 RPM)

"LOAD HANDLER™"

8 LHA 2022 R
8 LHA 2024 R

INT. (ATTACHED) REG.

AC
STA

REG.

BLACK

RED

B+ ⊕

⊖

YEL

STA
AC

VOLT
ADJ.

GREEN
F

GREEN
F

YELLOW
AC
STA

BLACK
—

RED
+

YELLOW
AC
STA

← EXCITE IF ALT. NEEDS

VOLT. REG. IS
8 RG 2023
OR
8 RG 2025

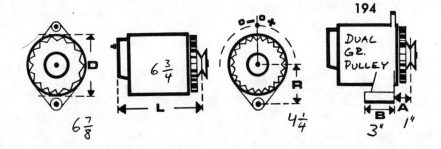

$6\frac{3}{4}$

$6\frac{7}{8}$

L

$4\frac{1}{4}$

R

DUAL GR. PULLEY

3"   B   A   1"

MOTOROLA

BRUSH ASSEMBLY
UNDER REAR COVER
(LOOKS LIKE REG).

12V 130A (5000 RPM)

8 LHA 2026 V

EXT. REG. *

(8 LHA 2028V IS SAME
EXCEPT BACK HOUSING
90° ROT. VS. FRONT;
ONE CAN BE MADE
INTO THE OTHER)

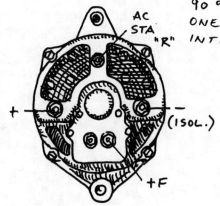

AC STA
"R"

+

— (ISOL.)

+F

* CAN BE CONVERTED TO SELF-EXCITED,
INT. (ATTACHED) REG. WITH MOTOROLA
KIT S-277 WHICH INCLUDES
REG. 8 RG 2026.

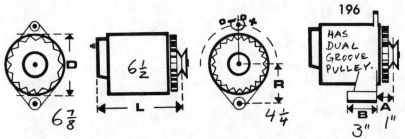

HAS DUAL GROOVE PULLEY.

$6\frac{7}{8}$

$6\frac{1}{2}$

$4\frac{1}{4}$

3"   1"

12V - 90A / 5000 RPM

8 LHA 2027R

MOTOROLA

"LOAD HANDLER™"

EXT. REG. *

(SELF-EXCITING*)

ENCLOSED, REMOV'BLE
BRUSH ASSEMBLY.
BIG BALL BEARINGS
EACH END.

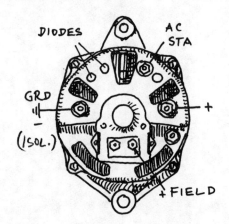

DIODES

AC STA

GRD

(ISOL.)

+

+ FIELD

* CAN BE CONVERTED TO INT., ATTACHED
REG. WITH MOTOROLA KIT 5-278 WHICH
INCLUDES REG. 8 RG 2023.

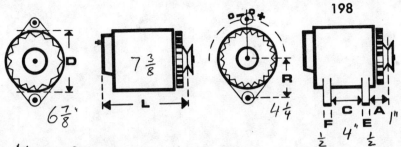

MOTOROLA   12V 130A
                 (AT 5000 RPM)
"LOAD HANDLER™" 90A AT 2000 RPM

                 8 LHA 2023 V

                 INT (ATTACHED) REG.
                     SELF-EXCIT.

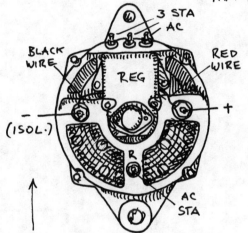

                 REG:
                 8 RG 2026

                 BRUSH HOLDER
                 UNDER REG.
                 BIG (25 MM) BALL
                 BEARINGS EACH
                 END.

CAN BE USED AS
NEG. GROUND,
ISOLATED GROUND,
OR POSITIVE GROUND ALT.

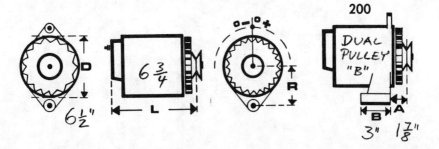

200

DUAL PULLEY "B"

6½"

6¾

L

R

3" 1⅞"

B A

MOTOROLA

CAST IRON HSG.

"SA" SERIES
12, 24, 32 V
12V: 85-120A
24/32V: 70A

INT (ATTACHED) REG.
(SHOWN), OR
EXT. REG.:
"F" TERMINAL.

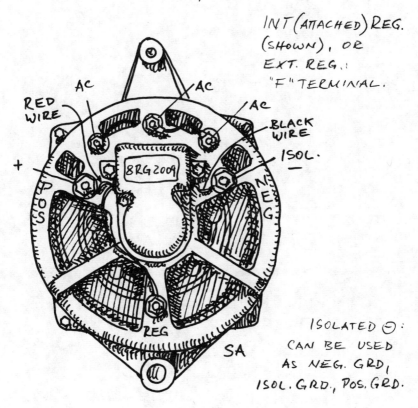

RED WIRE

AC   AC

AC

BLACK WIRE

ISOL.

+

8RG2009

POS

NEG

REG

SA

ISOLATED ⊖:
CAN BE USED
AS NEG. GRD,
ISOL. GRD, POS. GRD.

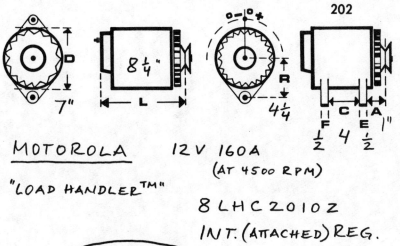

MOTOROLA   12V 160A
(AT 4500 RPM)

"LOAD HANDLER™"

8 LHC 2010 Z
INT. (ATTACHED) REG.

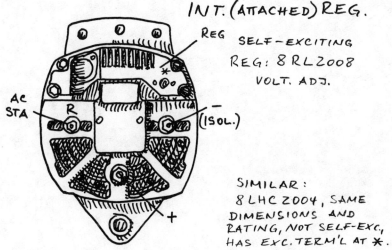

REG

SELF—EXCITING
REG: 8 RL 2008
VOLT. ADJ.

AC
STA

R

− (ISOL.)

+

SIMILAR:
8 LHC 2004, SAME
DIMENSIONS AND
RATING, NOT SELF-EXC.
HAS EXC. TERM'L AT *.

LOOKS SIMILAR TO 8 SB SERIES (BRUSHLESS)
BUT HAS BRUSHES, UNDER COVER AT CENTER.

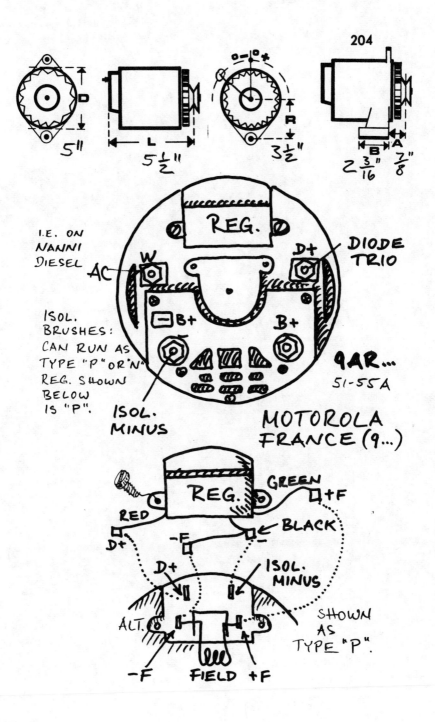

5"

L

5 ½"

3 ½"

R

2 3/16"   7/8"

B   A

REG.

I.E. ON
NANNI
DIESEL

AC

W

D+

DIODE
TRIO

ISOL.
BRUSHES:
CAN RUN AS
TYPE "P" OR "N".
REG. SHOWN
BELOW
IS "P".

B+

B+

ISOL.
MINUS

9AR...
51-55A

MOTOROLA
FRANCE (9...)

REG.

GREEN

+F

RED

BLACK

D+

-F

D+

ISOL.
MINUS

ALT.

SHOWN
AS
TYPE "P".

-F

FIELD +F

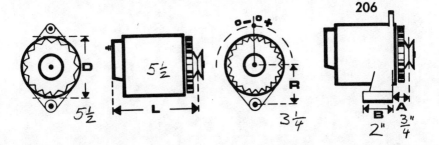

$5\frac{1}{2}$

$5\frac{1}{2}$ L $3\frac{1}{4}$ R   B   A   2" $\frac{3}{4}$"   D

MOTOROLA

TYPE P

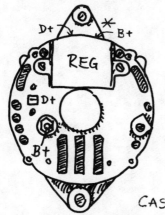

D+   ✳ B+

REG

D+

B+

9DA (MADE IN FRANCE)

12V 55A ("J" IN NUMBER)

12V 62A ("L" IN NUMBER)

INT (ATTACHED, FLUSH) REG. (SKETCHED), ALSO WITH EXT. REG.: "R" & "F" LUGS.

NO WIRES UNDER REG. PLUGS CONNECT TO D+ & F+, ALSO HAS LUGS ON TOP: ✳

CASE IS GRD., DIODE TRIO: D+

BRUSH HOLDER ACCESSIBLE UNDER REG.

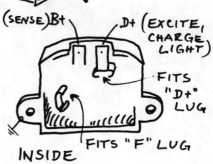

WITH EXT. REG.:
"R" AND "F" LUGS.

REG.
F → "F" ON ALT.
2 → "R" ON ALT.
3 → B+ SENSE
4 → CH. LT., EXCITE.
CASE → GROUND.

(SENSE) B+   D+ (EXCITE, CHARGE LIGHT)

FITS "D+" LUG

FITS "F" LUG

INSIDE OF REG.

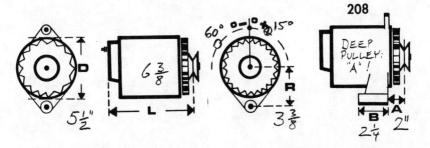

MOTOROLA 9BB (12V 55A) AND
9FB (12V 65A)
"9" IN NUMBER: MADE
IN FRANCE.

TYPE P

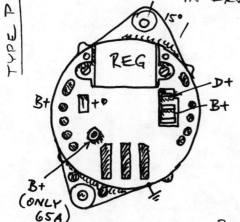

INT (ATTACHED FLUSH)
REG.
BRUSH HOLDER
UNDER REG., ONE
BRUSH ON GRD, OTHER
GREEN WIRE TO REG.
RED WIRE D+, LUG.

FIELD DIODES,
DIODE TRIO.

REG. CASE IS GRD
ALT. CASE GROUND.

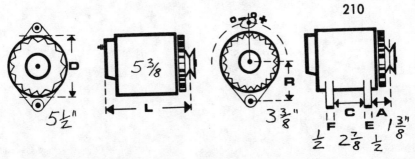

NIPPONDENSO   021000-42x

EXT. REG.

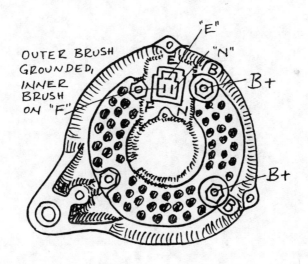

OUTER BRUSH
GROUNDED,
INNER
BRUSH
ON "F"

"E"

"N"

B+

B+

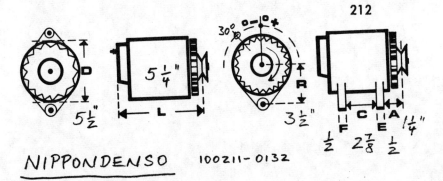

NIPPONDENSO   100211-0132

3 SCREW TERMINALS UNDER COVER:

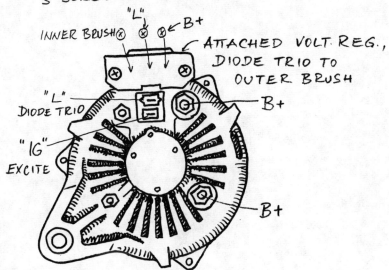

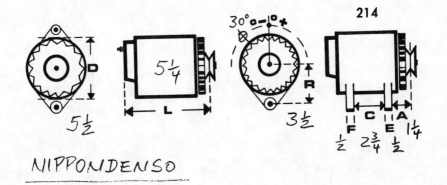

NIPPONDENSO

3 SCREW TERMINALS UNDER COVER:
- OUTER BRUSH ON "IG"
INNER BRUSH ON REG. — B+ (SENSE)
ATTACHED REG.

+12 V "IG"

"N"

AC STATOR

B+

B+

NO DIODE TRIO.

DIFFERENT: NO "L"!

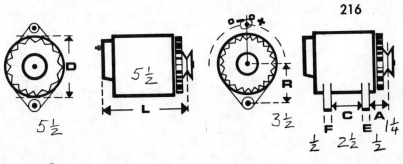

$5\frac{1}{2}$

$3\frac{1}{2}$

$\frac{1}{2}$ $2\frac{1}{2}$ $\frac{1}{2}$ $1\frac{1}{4}$

NIPPONDENSO

INT. REG.
DIODE TRIO

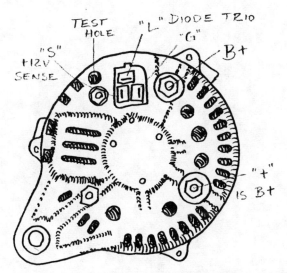

TEST HOLE

"L" DIODE TRIO

"G"

"S" +12V SENSE

B+

"+" IS B+

DIODE TRIO ON OUTER BRUSH,
INNER BRUSH ON REG. AND TAB
UNDER TEST HOLE

INDEX

AC, alternating current   2, 12, 13, 14
AC terminal   26, 27, 29, 61, 69, 146
A terminal   152, 170
Alternating current   2, 12, 13, 14
Alternator dimensions   114
    disassembling   92
    load, caution   109
    output voltage, caution   43
Ampere hour   43, 54
Automatic cutoff   57
Auxiliary diodes   28, 69, 86, 91, 97, 146
    and battery charging   29
AUX terminal   29, 40, 41, 146, 156, 166, 182, 184
Battery   43
    as filter   20, 31
    charging   50
    storage capacity   55
    switch   42
    voltage   36, 50
Bosch   33 Amp ext. reg.   120
       55 Amp ext. reg.   118
       55 Amp int. reg.   116
       65 Amp int. reg.   122, 124
Bridge rectifier   20
Brush, grounded   38
    holder, Hitachi   105
        Motorola   186
Brushless alternator   126, 128, 180, 202
Brush pin hole   94
Charge indicator light   34
    add a   111
Charging diodes   29, 42, 44
Charging light   40, 41
Chopped direct current   20
Coil   4, 10
    stator   98
Convert P to N   110
Current, battery charging   54
Cut in speed   65
Cycles per revolution   24

Darlington circuit 36
Definitions 38
Delco alternator models 126
  diode trio 62, 97
  external regulator 68, 70, 71
  internal regulator 50, 69, 91, 92, 105, 146
    and manual control 56
  P and N types 69
  voltage selector plug 70
  10DN series 136
  10SI-110 series with screen 142
  10SI-116 and 136 series 144
  20DN-100 series 132
  20DN-250 series 134
  17SI and 15SI series 138
  27SI-200 series 140
Delta stator coils 23
DF terminal 118, 120
Diagram 46, 47
Dimensions, alternator 114
Diode 19
  faulty 97
  test 19
  trio 62, 63
    Delco 146
    faulty 104
    test 86, 97
Diode, voltage adjusting 51
Diode voltage drop 45
Direct current 2
Disassembling alternator 92
Electromechanical regulator : see mechanical 38
Emergency repairs 102
E terminal 158
Excite 40, 64, 110
  current range 64, 65
  diode 41
  resistor 65
Field coil 8, 31, 36, 38, 40, 60, 69, 101
  test 82, 101
Field current 59
  emergency 108
  resistor 109
Field wire 105

Filter   20
Ford 60 Amp ext. reg.   148
Ford 65 Amp ext. reg.   150
Generator   2
Heat by diodes   28
Heat sink   27, 144, 146
Hitachi 35 Amp ext. reg.   152
         50 Amp ext. reg.   154
         50 Amp int. reg.   156
         50 Amp, 60 Amp int. reg.   158
Idiot light   34, 40, 41, 64, 65
    add an   111
Induction   3
Intermediate summary   17
Internal components, Delco   146
Internal regulator, faulty   105
Isolating diode   29, 61, 182
    faulty   104
    test   87
Lamp, also see test light   49
Lead acid battery   54
Leece-Neville   160, 162, 164
Load Handler, Motorola   192, 194, 196, 198, 202
L terminal   156, 158, 172, 176
Lucas 42 Amp int. reg.   166
Magnet   3
Magnetism, residual   64
Manual alternator controls   54
Marchal 60 Amp ext. reg.   168
Mechanical regulator   32
    two coil type   34
    voltage adjustment   33
    with manual alternator controls   56
Mitsubishi 35 Amp ext. reg.   170
            45 Amp int. reg.   172
            50 Amp int. reg.   174
            45 Amp int. reg.   178
            50 Amp ext. reg.   178
            65 Amp int. reg.   178
Motorola attached regulators 63, 66, 67, 68, 72
                    73, 188, 190, 192, 200, 204, 206

Motorola isolating diode 87, 88, 182
  external voltage regulator 66, 73, 184
  models description 180
  35 Amp, 55 Amp–6 V ext. reg. A, 8AL 184
  84 Amp int. reg. LHA 190
  90 Amp int. reg. 192
  130 Amp ext. reg. 194
  90 Amp ext. reg. 196
  130 Amp int. reg. 198
  85 Amp to 120 Amp int. reg. SA 200
  160 Amp int. reg. LHC 202
  51 Amp to 55 Amp int. reg. 9AR 204
  55 Amp to 62 Amp int. reg. 9DA 206
  55 Amp to 65 Amp int. reg. 9BB, 9FB 208
Nippondenso with ext. reg. 210
  ext. or int. reg. 212
  int. reg. 214
  int. reg. 216
NPN transistor 35
N type regulator 37, 59, 108
N terminal 152, 154, 170
Open main diode 102
Peak invert voltage rating, PIV, diodes 19
Percent of full battery charge 54
Permanent magnet 4, 7
Phase 14
Pilot light 34, 40, 41, 64, 65
Pin hole 93, 94, 95
PNP transistor 35
Positive ground 37, 128, 196, 198, 200, 202, 204
Power for field 28
P type regulators and alternators 37, 59, 108
P terminal 174, 176
Pulse 6
Rectified AC 14
Rectifier bridge, Delco 144, 146
Rectifying diode 19
  test 84
Regulator, voltage 7
  faulty 106
  uses AC 71, 72

Regulator, Ford internal — 99
  mechanical, Nippondenso — 76
  setting, voltage — 182
  test of voltage setting — 83
  types P or N — 38
  with relay — 72
Regulator, 3 terminal — 60
    Chrysler N — 77, 108
    Chrysler P — 107
    Delco — 63
    Lucas — 74
    Marchal — 75
    Motorola — 63
    plus terminal — 61
Regulator, 4 terminal
    Lucas — 74
    Motorola — 66
    Paris-Rhone — 76
    with excite resistor — 66, 67
Regulator, 5 terminal
    Delco N — 70
    Delco P — 68, 71
    Ford P — 73
    Ford with ammeter — 74
    Hitachi N — 77
    Motorola P — 67
Regulator, 6 terminal — 68
    Motorola N — 188
REG terminal — 61
Relay contacts — 34
Repairs — 79
Replacement regulator — 107
Resistor, excite — 40
Reverse voltage protection diode — 37
Ripple — 14
  test — 99
Rotor — 5, 8, 9
  test — 101
R terminal — 132, 136, 140, 144, 172, 176
  Delco — 146
RPM and voltage — 48

Schematic	46, 47
Self exciting	64
SEV Marchal 60 Amp ext. reg.	168
Shorted main diode	102
Silicon diode, rectifier	2, 19
Slip ring	9, 94, 101, 180
Smoothness	20
Solid state regulator, transistor function	35
Splitter diodes	44
STA terminal	148, 150
Stator	10, 11
connections, Delco	146
testing	98
windings	15, 16
S terminal	156, 158
Switch	42
Tachometer terminal, add a	111
Terminal, diode	20
"1" and "2" Delco	140, 144
"61"	168
Test hole	83, 91, 92, 172, 174, 176
Testing main diodes	96
stator coils	98
Test lamp	81, 82
Test, off engine	84
on engine	79
output	80
field current	80, 81
voltage regulator	89
type N	90
type P	91
Three phase alternating current	14, 21, 22
Three phase rectifier	26
Trouble shooting	79
Voltage adjustment plug, Delco	140
Voltage drop, at isolating diode	61
at charging diodes	44
compensating diode	45
Voltage regulator	
adjustment	50
and battery charging	43, 50

Voltage regulator : also see Regulator
Voltage regulator, electromechanical   31, 38
    function   31
    setting   51
    test, separately   49
    solid state   31, 38
    voltage setting   43
    testing in operation   48
    types   59
Voltage source, variable, for test   49
Voltmeter   48
Volt ohm meter VOM   82
    diode test   85
Watt   28
W terminal   122
Y stator coils   24
Zener diode   35